50 WAYS TO WEALTH

50 WAYS TO WEALTH

JOHN LOWE

Very best wishes

Gill & Macmillan

Gill & Macmillan Ltd
Hume Avenue, Park West, Dublin 12
with associated companies throughout the world
www.gillmacmillan.ie
© John Lowe 2008
978 07171 4383 2
Index compiled by Cover To Cover
Typography design by Make Communication
Print origination by O'K Graphic Design, Dublin
Printed and bound by Nørhaven Paperback A/S, Denmark

This book is typeset in 11/13.5 pt Minion LT.

The paper used in this book comes from the wood pulp of
managed forests. For every tree felled, at least one tree is
planted, thereby renewing natural resources.

A CIP catalogue record for this book is available from the
British Library.

5 4 3 2 1

CONTENTS

PREFACE

In February 2006 the columnist and television panellist Brendan O'Connor asked me to write a series of articles on making money for *LIFE*—the *Sunday Independent*'s weekly magazine—which he edits. Brendan wanted interesting articles that covered the mundane and the esoteric when it came to investing money, and he wanted them readable and engaging. The articles, which were published under the title 'Making Money with the Money Doctor', turned a boring subject into an attractive and eye-catching series, not least from Brendan's choice of accompanying photographs and racy headlines. The initial plan was for a thirteen-part series, but editorial and readers' responses were so positive that in the end it ran to seventy articles over eighteen months.

This book replicates fifty of the *LIFE* articles exactly as they appeared each Sunday in 2006 and 2007, confined by space constraints to approximately 1,000 words per article. While the theories and the philosophies of good investing never change, market conditions, such as legislation, interest rates and society mores, do change, so if you are going to consider an investment decision inspired by these articles you should first talk to your financial adviser or contact the Money Doctor directly to determine if changes have occurred.

The underlying philosophy behind the articles in this book is simple. Firstly, everyone has a right to become wealthy, and the more you believe this the more likely it is that it will happen for you. Secondly, knowledge is power, so if you arm yourself with financial information, wealth *will* come. For example, if you want to invest in art, buying the first painting that comes your way may not be the most prudent purchase. Researching the market for your preferred artist, taking plenty of advice and finding out where to obtain the best prices and best value will help you to reap rewards.

There have been many recent doom-and-gloom commentators on the Irish economy. For some, it would appear to be the quickest way to their fifteen minutes of fame. Is it part of the Irish psyche that we love to hear stories of people less fortunate than ourselves? *The Money Doctor* adopts a more positive attitude, no matter what obstacles arise. Remember, Ireland is now the second-wealthiest country in the world, and this has not happened by chance. Be grateful and praise the good things in Irish life rather than looking for the irritations. We have had a brilliant fifteen years financially in Ireland, with unprecedented growth, and there are even better days to come for those who have prepared and are patient.

In this book you have fifty ways of making money—proven ways that have made more than 36,000 millionaires in Ireland alone; fifty ways of making money in order to achieve one of your goals: wealth. If you have already reached that goal, you may wish to retain and preserve your wealth with further investment diversification, while if you have not, by buying this book, you are now potentially on the road to your first million!

I would sincerely like to thank the *Sunday Independent* and Brendan O'Connor for giving me the opportunity, Mary O'Sullivan for her introduction to Brendan, and the great *LIFE* team at the *Sunday Independent* for their fantastic support and talents. I would also like to thank my family, colleagues and fellow-advisers in Providence

Finance Services, friend and mentor Jonathan Self, along with north Cork's Gerry Murphy—entrepreneur, philanthropist and friend—for their unstinting support, and especially Fergal Tobin, publishing director, and the whole team at Gill & Macmillan for their enormous help and support with this, my fifth book.

Finally, let me repeat my earlier invitation: if you need clarification on any subject, or if you want to communicate for any reason, I would be delighted to hear from you. Enjoy, and I wish you good health, wealth and happiness.

February 2008
E-mail info@moneydoctor.ie
Website www.moneydoctor.ie

01 | ONE HOT PROPERTY
SYNDICATES

If you have always yearned to become a property magnate, buying and selling multi-million-euro buildings for vast profits, but assumed you didn't have the capital to get started, then think again. Because, thanks to the growing popularity of property syndicates, it is now possible for private investors with as little as €20,000 to double and even treble their money in a relatively short period, with little or no risk.

A property syndicate is simply a group of investors who pool their money in order to buy a much more valuable building (or series of buildings) than they would otherwise be able to afford.

The best way to explain the concept is with a real-life example.

I am involved with a property company that concentrates on grade A commercial property in one of the fastest-growing countries in Europe: Romania, which joins the European Union next year.

In February 2005 we got wind of an office building that had come up for sale in the heart of Bucharest for €6½ million. It was a fantastic deal. The building was in a great location, well maintained and fully let. Indeed its tenants were all blue-chip companies, like Rank Xerox, paying a staggering €800,000+ a year in rent; that's an annual return of over 12%. I formed a syndicate with eleven other people, and we had no trouble persuading a bank to lend us three-quarters of the purchase price. This left us the deposit to find: €185,000 each. Some of my fellow-investors had the cash available, but for those who didn't I arranged mortgages on their existing property. Before we had even finished buying the building another interested purchaser came along and offered us a €2 million profit to sell our interest. We said no to a €166,000 instant gain *each*, because we knew there would be bigger profits to come. The rent from our tenants more than covers the syndicate's loan costs; and we are looking forward to some really juicy capital gains in the future.

Personally, I believe Romania is one of the best places in Europe for this sort of deal, but only if you can find a suitable property and covenant. At the moment I am considering two similar projects in Bucharest that, I hope, will show similar (if not better) returns.

One of the really good things about property syndicates is that there is so much choice available. However, you must be ready to act quickly, as the better deals get snapped up in a matter of weeks and sometimes even days.

Property investments are judged on the following factors:

1. **The yield.** This is the amount of rent in relation to the property's value. If the property is worth €1 million and the rent is €40,000 a year, then the yield is 4%.
2. **The potential for capital gain.** Will the building go up in value, and if so, by how much and how quickly?
3. **The risk.** It is usually (but not always) true that the lower the yield the lower the risk. If you are buying

retail property, then a large shop with a long-established tenant in Grafton Street, Dublin, is going to be safer than a small convenience store in a suburb of Galway—but not necessarily as lucrative.

4. **The exit mechanism.** How long will your money be tied up for? Usually it is a minimum of five years, but it could be a minimum of ten years. Bear in mind that most syndicates do not pay out any income from rent received. So, if you borrow money (for instance by taking out a second mortgage) to buy into a syndicate you will have to cover this cost yourself until the syndicate sells the property.

5. **The promoters.** You need to be certain that the company promoting and managing the syndicate is reputable, experienced and financially secure.

Incidentally, property professionals assess each deal according to something called the *internal rate of return* (IRR). The IRR is calculated by adding together the annual yield with the likely annual capital gain. The higher the IRR the better the deal; but you need to be wary of promoters who over-promise.

If you are serious about joining a property syndicate, then I would strongly recommend doing some background research. Is the property in good condition? Is it in a good location? Is the country where it is located politically stable? Does it have (or will it be easy to find) reliable tenants? You should take professional legal and financial advice before signing anything.

Thanks to low interest rates, borrowing to invest in a property syndicate can make sound financial sense. If you had €50,000 in savings and borrowed €150,000 you would have €200,000 to put into a suitable syndicate. If the syndicate produced an IRR of 20% a year for each of the

first five years, you would see a total return of over
€500,000 by 2011. That's a 150% profit on your original
investment—considerably more than you could hope for if
you left your money on deposit with a bank or building
society.

(First published 19 February 2006)

02 | A GAME OF TRUST
SELF-DIRECTED TRUSTS

I t is a mystery to me why so many of Ireland's property millionaires move abroad to offshore tax havens in order to avoid tax when all they really need to do is set up a self-directed trust. These fantastically generous, underutilised schemes are ideal for company directors, business owners and senior employees who want to (*a*) slash their income-tax bills and (*b*) invest in property without having to pay tax on the profits. A similar and equally generous scheme is also available for sole traders, such as solicitors and accountants.

A self-directed trust is a type of pension—a *small self administered pension scheme* (SSAP), in fact, to give it its proper name. It is like any other pension scheme in that

- contributions into your trust are tax-free. So, if you pay tax at the higher rate of 42%, a €100 a month investment will only cost you €58
- any profits made in the trust are completely tax-free.

Where a self-directed trust really comes into its own, however, is as follows:

- You can invest a considerably higher percentage of your total annual income tax-free than you would be able to with a normal personal pension—up to 150% of your annual income at the age of forty, for instance, and up to 250% of your annual income at the age of fifty. What's more, the highest sum you can contribute is set at €5 million, which is a lot of money to be able to invest tax-free.

- You could start accessing your money as young as age fifty.
- You can vary the amount you put into your trust from year to year.
- There is much greater flexibility regarding the choice of investments. In particular, these schemes are ideal for investing in property.
- Your trust can 'gear' to further boost its profits. In plain English, this means the trust can borrow money to invest—up to three times the amount held.

This last feature, introduced in the Finance Act (2004), is what really makes self-directed trusts so attractive.

Let me give you a real-life example of how I helped one of my clients to take advantage of a self-directed trust.

On my advice, Jim, a businessman, set up a self-directed trust into which he made sufficient contributions to do a lucrative British property deal. Last year the trust bought a well-appointed and well-maintained office building in Leicester, let to the British government at an annual rental income of 7% of the purchase price. The total cost of the purchase, including expenses, was £960,000, financed with a twenty-year loan of £648,000 (70% LTV) at 6%. In other words, the rent from the building is £64,750 a year, but the annual loan cost is only £55,709.64—meaning an annual profit of around £9,000 a year. All the rent is tax-free. All the mortgage payments are tax-free, as they are deemed pension contributions. And when the building is sold, any gain is also tax-free.

When you also bear in mind that Jim's initial

contribution—which converted to £312,000—was tax-free you can see why I am so enthusiastic about self-directed trusts.

Incidentally, there is another important benefit attached to self-directed trusts. When you retire you can take 25% of the value of the fund as a tax-free lump sum. The balance can be placed in an *approved retirement fund* (ARF), which could, if you want, be re-invested back into another property deal. (Another reason to use an ARF to manage your money after you retire is that it will offer a way to pass on your assets to your family.)

What else should you watch out for? Pensions legislation is complicated, so you should take specialist advice before taking any action. Also, if you were thinking of putting your self-directed trust money into a holiday home or vintage wine, you will be disappointed, as the investment rules are quite strict.

Setting up a self-directed trust is inexpensive. You should budget around €4,000 in fees (including VAT) and allow annual management costs of between 1% and 1½%, depending on the size of the fund.

If you are a sole trader (e.g. accountant, solicitor, doctor), by the way, you can still avail of most of the benefits I have described above, but you will be doing so using a *self-invested personal pension*.

If you are a business owner, company director or senior employee and you want to slash your income-tax bill and make a tax-free property investment, nothing (not even moving to an offshore tax haven) beats the advantages offered by a self-directed trust—especially as you can gear your investments to further boost your profits.

(First published 26 February 2006)

03 | THE FRENCH CONNECTION
FRENCH LEASE-BACK PROPERTIES

Can you find at least €20,000 to invest? Could you spare a further €400 or so a month? Then I strongly recommend that you consider putting your money into a 'French leaseback'. Made possible by the generosity of the French government, leasebacks offer you the potential of a substantial capital gain with none of the risk normally associated with property investment.

The word 'leaseback' makes this opportunity sound more complicated than it actually is. Basically, what you will be doing is buying a French property (with the aid of a loan) to be let out to holidaymakers. This would make sound financial sense even without the two extra reasons I am going to tell you about in a moment. France is the most popular holiday destination in the whole world; it is also a G8 economy; and its property market has been rising steadily. Over the last five years, for instance, prices have grown by 87%—that's roughly 17% a year. Most important of all, demand for holiday property still outstrips supply.

It was this shortage that caused the French government to step in and offer not one but two incredible incentives designed to stimulate investment. Firstly, if you purchase a new or refurbished property you will get all the VAT refunded—in effect reducing the price by 19.6%. Secondly, French property management companies (PMCS) are now allowed to offer a guaranteed rental income based on the cost of the property for up to eleven years. Some companies are actually offering a staggering 5.99% guaranteed on the net value until 2017.

In other words, you can buy property at a substantial discount; you stand to make a tasty capital gain, assuming prices continue to rise; and—best of all—your rental income is guaranteed. It is this last feature that is particularly attractive to private investors. Instead of having to worry about finding tenants and managing your property you can sit back and collect a guaranteed income.

Let's consider a typical example: an apartment being offered by France's biggest PMC, established for over forty years and listed on the Paris Bourse. The total cost is €304,000, to include VAT, furnishings and legal costs. However, after receiving your VAT refund of €49,000 the net cost to you is €255,000. Your guaranteed return for the next eleven years is 4.5% a year on the net property value. To fund your purchase you put down a deposit of €22,270 and take out a French twenty-year repayment mortgage for €243,000 (that's 80% of the €304,000) at a current rate of 3.5%. The net effect of this arrangement is that you receive €11,250 a year in rent but pay out a little over €16,900 in capital and interest—leaving you a monthly shortfall to find of some €472.

In other words, with €22,270 and a monthly commitment of €472 you stand to make the full capital gain on a property that would normally have cost you over €300,000! Best of all, hold on to the property for twenty years and you will own it outright. Imagine how much that will be worth to you!

So, what factors should you take into account before investing in a French leaseback? Here are some things to consider:

- It is important to choose a well-established PMC. You don't want to deal with any firm that might go bankrupt.
- Look out for extra perks. The PMC I mentioned above offers its investors a 30% rental discount on all its holiday accommodation in other locations.
- Bear in mind that this will be an investment: you can't opt to live in the property yourself.
- The full VAT refund is made by the French government on the assumption that you will hold on to the property for at least twenty years. If you sell the property before the twenty years are up you will have to pay the VAT back on a pro-rata basis.
- The VAT refund can take a few months to receive, but a well-established PMC will cover the cost for you, so that you don't have to find the extra money at the start.
- Remember, inheritance laws are different in France. You should take legal advice before deciding to buy.
- Although there is a dual tax agreement in force between Ireland and France, you should also take tax advice.
- Some leasebacks are on properties with two-year completion dates. You may have to part-fund the construction on a stage-payment basis. French banks will bridge this at a competitive rate.
- Rent will be paid to you annually and in arrears. Depending on when you buy, you could have to wait a whole year for your first rental payment.
- To take out a mortgage in France you will have to show that you can afford the monthly repayments, just as you would in Ireland.

Before you make any major financial decision you should always take professional advice. However, if you are looking for a long-term, above-average capital gain with relatively low risk, I doubt you will find an investment opportunity that beats a well-chosen French leaseback.

(First published 5 March 2006)

04 | GET INTO BONDAGE

INVESTING IN BONDS

One guaranteed way to make sure that your money continues to grow, regardless of any external threats to your wealth—such as a falling stock market, lower property prices or a recession—is to invest in bonds. Once the preserve of the super-rich, nowadays someone with as little as €1,000 to spare can take advantage of the fantastic profit opportunities and cast-iron security they offer.

What exactly is a bond? When governments, companies and other big organisations (such as the World Bank) need to borrow money they often do so by selling or 'issuing' bonds. Each bond has a

maturity date: this is the date when the investors get paid back their capital. This might be in five, ten, twenty years' time or more

face value: this is the amount the bond cost when it was first issued. Typical face values would be €1,000, €5,000 or €10,000.

Most bonds entitle the holder to a fixed amount of interest, referred to as the *coupon*. The coupon is usually paid quarterly, bi-annually or annually. On the maturity date the bondholder will then be paid back the face value.

For example, if you purchased a newly issued €10,000 twenty-year bond paying a 5% coupon you would receive an annual income of €500 for twenty years, and then you would get your original €10,000 back.

Some bonds, however, known as *zero coupon bonds,* don't pay out regular interest but instead guarantee you a larger, fixed amount on maturity. Either way, one of the most important features of bonds is that they can be bought and sold any time between when they are issued and the maturity date.

After a bond has been issued it may be worth more, less or the same as its face value. This means that in addition to earning interest from your bonds you can choose to buy and sell them for profit.

The value of a bond will depend on a variety of factors, including interest rates, inflation, the level of risk (a bond issued by the Chilean government, for example, would be considered riskier than a bond issued by the Irish government), the size of the coupon and the length of time until the bond reaches maturity.

As an investor, bonds offer you three extremely valuable benefits:

1. Income. Bonds provide a regular income until the maturity date—making them one of the few investments that pay a guaranteed return for a fixed period.

2. Diversification. Wise investors divide their money up between different types of investment—property, a pension, stocks and shares and so forth—in order to reduce their risk and optimise their profits. This is called diversification. Bonds are an ideal way to diversify. One reason for this is that when other markets are doing badly, the price of bonds tends to rise. Another is that they offer a high level of security.

3. Protection. Historically bonds have protected investors from many of the problems that can beset the economy, including inflation, deflation, recession, falling property prices and a weak stock market. This is because bonds offer investors the security of a guaranteed income without any risk to their capital.

The secret to investing in this sector is to build up a portfolio of bonds offering different maturity dates and different rates of return. If you want to boost your profits further then re-invest both your coupons and, on maturity, your capital back into new bonds. There is plenty of choice, including the following:

Government bonds. Issued by national governments such as the United States, Britain, Germany and Ireland. These are virtually risk-free—hence the expression 'gilt-edged' investment.

Emerging-market bonds. Issued by countries with developing economies, such as Russia or Thailand. These carry slightly more risk but pay a higher return.

Local government bonds—known in the United States as 'municipal bonds'—which are issued by local governments, primarily in Europe and America.

Corporate bonds. Issued by larger companies and multinationals.

Mortgage-backed and asset-backed securities. The process of *securitisation*, whereby banks and other financial institutions 'bundle' up their customers' debts (including mortgages) and sell them on, has led to a new sort of bond.

Junk bonds. Issued by companies that are considered to be high-risk. The return can look attractive—but, of course, you may never receive your coupons or capital on maturity.

There is a thriving market in bonds (estimated at being worth as much as $118 trillion), and no-one who is serious about making money can afford to ignore the huge potential for profit. You can buy bonds directly from the issuer or you can go to a specialist bond manager. Naturally, before investing you should take professional advice.

(First published 19 March 2006)

05 | WHAT A BEAUTY!
INVESTING IN FINE ART

Are you interested in the idea of buying a work of art, enjoying it for a period and then selling it for a substantial gain? There is no doubt that it can be done. Prices for individual artists can rise quickly. Almost any piece by Andy Warhol, for instance, would have shown a 600% gain over the last decade. Even the Irish property market hasn't grown by that much!

However, investing in art is a complicated and high-risk enterprise. You should only undertake it if you have already built up a portfolio of other, more secure investments (such as shares, bonds and property) and can afford to tie your money up for the medium to long term. Bear in mind too that this is a market where knowledge is vital. The more you study it, the greater your chances of success.

According to the news service Bloomberg, the international art market is at present worth a staggering $5 trillion a year. Though largely fuelled by private collectors, a number of financial institutions have diversified a small percentage of their assets into art. The most famous of these is the British Rail Pensions Fund, which between the mid-1970s and mid-1990s invested 2.9% of its holdings in art, producing an annual return of 11.3%.

Art, like gold, vintage wine, or antiques, is referred to as an 'alternative investment'. The big disadvantage of such investments is that prices can fluctuate wildly and you won't always be able to sell when you want to. If you are buying art as an investment (as opposed to buying it purely for pleasure) you should focus on established artists. Whether they are living or dead, there should be a wide market and strong demand for their work. One good test is the number of books written about the artist, another is how many dealers sell their work. Any artist who doesn't come up for sale regularly at one of the major auction houses will be too high a risk to consider a reasonable investment.

If you have a minimum of $250,000 to spare you could consider investing in the Fine Art Fund in London, a unit trust managed by a former finance director of Christie's, which produced a return of 54% last year. Otherwise, if you are interested in putting some of your money into art, my advice would be to consider original prints.

An original print is a work of art that has been reproduced, almost always under the artist's supervision, a limited number of times. Modern and contemporary prints will be signed and numbered by the artist; older prints may not be.

Prints offer an opportunity to own work by the most famous names in art history at a relatively low cost. You can buy a Picasso, a Hockney or a Rembrandt print for under €15,000—a fraction of what you would pay for a painting by any of these great artists. Take, for instance, the artist Howard Hodgkin, now being shown in the Irish Museum of Modern Art. One of his oil paintings would set you back at least €300,000, whereas a recent etching can be had for around €9,000.

Because the modern and contemporary art market, with

its speculative investment potential, has been growing so fast, it is the sector that attracts the majority of print buyers. Certainly anyone who invested even as recently as two or three years ago in prints by almost any well-known modern artist you care to name, from Joan Miró to Lucian Freud, will have experienced spectacular gains. Nevertheless, older artists—especially such famous printmakers as Albrecht Dürer, Andrea Mantegna, Rembrandt van Rijn and William Hogarth—may make better financial sense. Works by these artists are not prone to the vagaries of fashion, demand is always strong, and prices have been increasing steadily over the last hundred years.

When buying prints, investors are faced with a choice of going to a dealer or bidding at auction. To get a good feel for both, why not visit London in the last week of March? Close to fifty dealers will be displaying their wares at the 21st London Original Print Fair, to be held at the Royal Academy (00 44 207 4392000), 22–26 March. At the same time you could visit Bonham's of Bond Street (00 44 207 4477447), Sotheby's of Bond Street (00 44 207 2935000) and Christie's of King Street, all of which are holding major print sales on 23 March, 28 March and 29 March, respectively.

Thanks to the internet, it is very easy to work out what you should be paying for a given print. A number of sites specialise in providing pricing information, including www.artprice.com, which covers more than 309,000 artists and 2,900 auction houses, and www.artnet.com, which covers more than 180,000 artists and will provide you with a precise valuation for any work you want to buy or sell. Remember, if you buy from a dealer they can usually be persuaded to offer a discount. 10% is the industry norm.

Finally, I recommend that you buy art you really like. If

the market doesn't go the way you expect, at least you'll be able to take pleasure from owning it. Do remember, art investment is high-risk. Take professional advice if you are uncertain whether it is for you.

(First published 20 March 2006)

06 | PRECIOUS METALS
INVESTING IN GOLD

If the so-called 'gold bugs'—investors who believe passionately in the long-term value of buying gold—are right, then this could be a good time to add a little glitter to your portfolio. Over the last five years the price of gold has more than doubled, from $250 to $660 a troy ounce, and it is still nowhere near its 1980 record of $850 a troy ounce.

Just because gold is cheap now when compared with twenty-five years ago doesn't automatically mean that it is a good investment. However, there are three sound reasons to believe that prices will continue to soar.

Firstly, the growing economies of Asia and the Middle East have resulted in a huge surge in demand—especially for gold jewellery. For proof one need look no further than global gold jewellery sales, which increased by 19% last year.

Secondly, a rising number of private investors all over the world have been putting some or all of their savings into gold as a hedge against economic or political instability and, in some cases, war. When investors feel the future is uncertain (as many appear to at the moment) the demand for gold always surges. This is doubtless in no small part due to the fact that the price of gold tends to move in the opposite direction to virtually all other conventional asset classes—making it ideal when investors wish to diversify.

Thirdly, the mining industry can't keep up with demand. Last year's figures show that in excess of 4,000 tonnes of gold were purchased, but only 2,500 tonnes were mined. What's more, production is falling by an average of 4% a year, and it will take the industry anything up to ten years to increase supply by the required volume. In the past, when demand outstripped supply, the shortfall was met by many of the world's central banks. No longer. Countries that had been disposing of their gold reserves have slowed down sales or even stopped selling altogether. Some central banks, notably those of Russia, Iran and China, are actually believed to be buying bullion.

Although I believe that gold prices are likely to carry on moving upward, I would only suggest buying if you already have a range of other investments, including shares, bonds and property. Furthermore, I would strongly advise against buying gold coins or gold bars. The idea of owning a little 'hoard' of gold may seem attractive. However, gold in all its forms is expensive to ship, store and insure. Instead I would recommend investing in one of the various gold mutual funds. These offer a cost-effective, convenient and potentially more lucrative way to benefit from any increase in gold's value.

A good example of what a mutual gold fund has to offer is the top-performing Merrill Lynch Gold and General Fund, which has produced an average annualised gain of 33.9% over the past five years and now is up around 1,000% since its launch in 1988. The bulk of the £855 million fund is invested in gold-mining shares. Obviously, gold-mining shares rise in line with the value of gold. Your risk is diversified and you can leave it to the fund manager to choose the best opportunities. There are plenty of funds to choose from, and you can pick a fund that matches your own objectives. One fund might aim to track the price of gold, for instance, another to track one of the various market indices, such as the FTSE mining index.

Speaking of the FTSE mining index, which outperformed the FTSE all-share index in 2005, if you have plenty of capital at your disposal an alternative option would be to buy a portfolio of individual mining company shares. On the upside, this will give you greater control and involvement. On the downside, you will have to decide which of the hundreds of different mining company shares to buy.

There is one further possibility worth considering. Invest your money in one of the exchange-traded funds (ETFs) for gold. An ETF is listed on the stock market and allows you full exposure to the price of gold without actually having to take delivery of the bullion. The fund buys and holds the gold, while the investor holds ETF shares. The world's biggest ETF is Exchange Traded Gold (marketed under different names), which holds 431 tonnes of the yellow metal. This is more than the Bank of England's reserves.

Incidentally, if you are planning to invest in gold it is worth noting that it can be held in self-administered pension schemes (SSAPs), or self-directed trusts for company owners, directors and senior executives, which could mean some tasty tax savings, depending on your circumstances.

One of the most senior industry experts in the world, Robert McEwen of US Gold, was recently reported as predicting that gold prices may reach $2,000 an ounce by 2010. If he is right you could be kicking yourself for not getting into the market while prices are still relatively low.

(First published 2 April 2006)

07 BE GOOD, BABY
ETHICAL INVESTMENTS

A re you interested in the idea of making lots of money and, at the same time, making the world a better place? You are not alone. A recent survey of Irish savers found that more than half are keen to put their cash into ethical investments. Indeed, ethical and socially responsible investment funds are one of the fastest-growing areas of personal finance. Such funds pool investors' money and then use it to buy shares in companies that meet defined criteria. For example, one fund might only invest in companies that behave in an environmentally responsible way, while another might focus on companies that aren't involved in the exploitation of people or animals.

The history of ethical investment can be traced back to the nineteenth century. It began when religious movements, most noticeably the Quakers and Methodists, recommended that their adherents withhold investment from companies that didn't embrace temperance and fair employment conditions. Over the course of the twentieth century the use of ethical criteria when choosing between investment options spread—especially among churches, charities and non-profit organisations. In 1971 the first ethical investment fund, the World Pax Fund, was founded with the declared objective of not supporting companies that were profiting from the Viet Nam war. During the 1980s opposition to the apartheid regime in South Africa and environmental concerns gave ethical investment a boost, and many more funds were established. By the new millennium close to a sixth of all US funds were invested in 'companies with a high degree of social responsibility.'

If you plan to adopt an ethical investment strategy, the first step is to consider what issues matter to you. Some of the corporate activities you may not wish to profit by include animal testing, genetic engineering, environmental destruction, inattention to human rights, intensive farming, nuclear power, arms, pesticides, pornography, deforestation, alcohol, tobacco, and low pay or poor conditions for workers. By the same token there may be specific activities or industries you wish to support through your investment. These could include companies with a good record of community involvement, environmental care, corporate governance and generous treatment of employees and suppliers. You may also decide to put your money into companies that provide 'positive' goods and services, such as organic food or health care.

Discovering whether a particular company—including a bank—meets your ethical criteria can be difficult and time-consuming. Indeed, one of the many advantages offered by ethical and socially responsible investment funds is that they have the resources to research and assess individual companies. Many funds supplement their knowledge with data from other sources, such as the British charity Ethical Investment Research Service (EIRIS). EIRIS, which offers a great deal of invaluable information through its web site (www.eiris.org), carries out independent research covering more than forty different areas and holds detailed, up-to-date information on more than 2,600 companies. Another

British non-profit body offering a range of invaluable information is the UK Social Investment Forum (www.uksif.org), which runs an excellent seminar programme.

One of the most prevalent myths concerning ethical investment is that the profit element will be less than if you invested without taking ethical considerations into account. If you look at the overall statistics, ethical funds have produced above-average returns, even allowing for the costs of extra screening. Many funds perform even better.

There are various reasons for this. Ethical fund managers study the companies they are considering investing in much more rigorously than their non-ethical colleagues. Also, companies with strong ethical principles tend to be better run and less hampered by regulatory, legal and publicity problems. In fact five ethical indices created by EIRIS to evaluate returns in the ethical investment sector produced financial returns almost exactly equivalent to the FTSE All-Share Index; the Investment Management Association found that ethical funds have matched or bettered the performance of similar non-ethical funds; and a Europe-wide study by the University of Maastricht made identical findings.

In Britain, Europe and the United States there are hundreds of ethical and socially responsible investment funds to choose from—so many that you can select funds that meet your precise investment needs in relation to risk and return. Furthermore, many of the ethical funds have now been established for more than two decades, allowing investors to analyse the long-term performance figures. Here in Ireland the options are still relatively limited, but many of our larger financial institutions—including First Active, Friends First, Standard Life, Hibernian and Dolmen Butler Briscoe/Dolmen Securities—now have ethical funds, and the choice is growing all the time. It is also possible, of course, to build up a portfolio of individual company shares.

As with any investment decision, you should take professional advice before taking action, the more so as you will want your planned investment to meet your ethical as well as your profit objectives.

(First published 9 April 2006)

08 GILTY PLEASURES
INVESTING IN GILTS—STOCKS AND SHARES

Of all the different long-term investment options open to you, nothing, not even property, is likely to make you juicier profits than buying publicly quoted stocks and shares. The British stock market, for instance, produced an average annual return of 9.6% a year between 1900 and 2005; the American stock market produced 11% a year between 1926 and 1999; and here at home, from 1974 up to 2006 the annual return averaged 17.4%.

These figures relate, of course, to the *average* annual return. Some investors will have done better than the market, others less well. The essential point is, however, that with planning and patience the stock market represents an incredible money-making opportunity.

The first question you need to consider is your overall stock market strategy. If you have sufficient capital to buy shares in a range of companies, and if you are interested in participating in the buying and selling decisions, then I would recommend 'direct' investment, that is to say, buying individual company shares. This has four clear benefits:

1. You will actually own a 'share' of the company you are investing in.

2. You will be entitled to a regular share of any profits. This income is known as the 'dividend'.
3. You can spread your risk—and maximise your gains— by buying shares in a range (or 'portfolio') of companies.
4. Your investment is 'liquid'—in other words, you can sell some or all of your shares any time you want.

The world's most successful investor is Warren Buffet, who turned every $10,000 his original investors provided him with in 1957 into more than $400 million today. His advice to private investors is simple: 'Buy low, sell high, bet big only when you know something the others don't, avoid popular fads, and don't trade very much, as the transaction costs will kill your returns.' He concedes that it is not an easy formula to follow, especially as we all have a natural urge to 'get busy.' Buffet is slow to invest in a share, spending years researching a company before making any decision; but once he has bought, he rarely sells.

Studying the tactics of investors like Buffet, it is clear that you can dramatically increase your chances of stock market gains by following a number of simple rules.

To begin with, do your homework. Learn everything you can about a company. Look at its annual reports to shareholders (available free), search on line for relevant news stories, read up on the sector in which it operates and its competitors. If possible, talk to people who work for the company. Bill Mann of motleyfool.com (a web site for investors), for example, bought shares in the failing Delta Airlines after chatting with flight crews and discovering that they were willing to accept a pay cut to keep the company going. His investment increased in value by 127% in three months!

A successful fund manager, Peter Lynch (author of an

excellent book called *Learn to Earn*), says this on the subject of gathering information: 'Every time you shop in a store, eat a hamburger, or buy new sunglasses, you're getting valuable input. By browsing around you can see what's selling and what isn't. By watching your friends, you know which computers they are buying, which brand of soda they are buying, whether Reeboks are in or out.' Lynch, incidentally, produced a total return of 2,700% between 1977 and 1990.

Secondly, have clear investment objectives. Are you interested in generating an income? If you are, you should invest in highly profitable companies that follow a policy of declaring generous dividends. Are you interested in long-term capital gain? If you are, you should invest in companies that are more likely to stand the tests of time. You also need to consider what degree of risk you are willing to endure. If a share price goes up you will clearly make money, but if the company does less well than expected or the market as a whole falls, then your investment could be worth less than you paid for it.

Thirdly, remember to diversify. If all your money is in one company, or one sector, or one country, then you increase your risk. The ideal is to build up a portfolio of shares that meet your objectives and spread your risk.

Fourthly, don't be tempted to trade too frequently. While share-dealing costs have come down substantially, making it less expensive to buy and sell small quantities of shares, charges can quickly eat into your profits. Also, the more times you buy and sell the less you will actually know about the company you are investing in.

Finally, educate yourself about the stock market, and make sure you know how to read the financial pages of the newspapers. At the bottom of this article I have listed some useful sources of information.

If you do decide to invest I would suggest starting with Irish companies. The Irish Stock Exchange (one of the oldest in the world, dating from 1793) offers a good range of opportunities and, thanks to the Celtic Tiger, has shown steady gains. The ISEQ Overall (our equivalent to the FTSE All-Share Index) stood at 1,000 on 4 January 1988 and recently went through the 8,000 mark—an 800% gain in eighteen years!

Do remember that you should discuss your overall financial position with a professional adviser before you start investing in the stock market. He or she will be able to recommend a good stockbroker (the 'big five' plus on-line brokers such as sharewatch.com) and will also help you to avoid paying any unnecessary tax on your gains.

One useful web site is that of the Irish Stock Exchange (www.ise.ie), which contains lots of information and tips. I deal with *investment clubs* in a later article.

(First published 30 April 2006)

09 | NOVEL IDEAS
COLLECTING FIRST EDITION BOOKS

If the idea of making money from a hobby appeals to you, then you should start collecting first-edition books.

Let me give you a real-life example. If you had bought a copy of the Nobel laureate Seamus Heaney's first collection of poetry, *Death of a Naturalist*, in 1999 you would have paid less than €500. Today the same book would sell for at least €2,000, giving you the double satisfaction of owning a valuable, rare and famous book and of making a 400% profit in less than seven years. Nor is this a one-off fluke. Experienced book collectors will tell you that with careful planning it is possible to regularly earn above-average returns from this fascinating and enjoyable hobby. However, as with any 'alternative' investment, caution is advisable. You shouldn't invest money you may need back in a hurry or that you can't afford to lose.

Books become valuable for a variety of reasons. To begin with, the author must be in demand. Collectability is strongly influenced by fashion and circumstances. Immediately after John Banville's *The Sea* won the Man Booker Prize, first editions of the book—previously available for less than €50—started changing hands for €200 and above. When Francis Ford Coppola made a film of another great Irish classic, Bram Stoker's *Dracula*, first editions increased tenfold in value, from around €1,000 to €10,000. Not that a film version guarantees success. First editions of *Captain Corelli's Mandolin* by Louis de Bernières regularly sold for €1,000 before the film bombed at the box office in 2001, whereas now they barely make half this price.

Interest in an author is not enough. The book itself must be what collectors call a first edition. A best-selling book will be printed many times in different formats. With very few exceptions, the only version that will be of value is the first printing of a book that is offered for sale. Over the years millions of copies of *Ulysses* have been printed, but it is the initial 1,000 run—published on James Joyce's fortieth birthday, 2 February 1922, in Paris—that are worth the most money. Furthermore, of this edition it is the 100 books signed by the author that command the highest prices.

Condition is another crucially important factor. If a book has been damaged or repaired or—in the case of modern novels—no longer has its jacket, the price will tumble. A signed first edition, on the other hand, will push the value up. This is especially true if there is a connection between the author and the recipient. Interestingly, rarity may have little or no effect on price. Speak to someone who specialises in antique books and you will discover that seventeenth and eighteenth-century leather-bound volumes, of which few copies may exist, are frequently worth only a few euros. By the same token, a relatively modern book that failed to sell, despite being a first edition and in short supply, is likely to be of no value.

In summary:

- Always choose books you will enjoy owning. This way

you will never regret your purchase.

- Only buy first editions. All other editions are relatively worthless.
- Buy books in the best condition you can afford. If you are buying new, modern first editions do not read the books. Unread books are worth more.
- Remember, rare does not automatically mean desirable.

What sort of books should you buy? Most dealers will advise you to specialise in a particular area. For instance, the value of literature related to medical discoveries is on the way up. Twenty years ago a signed offprint (a separate printing of an article) written by James Watson and Francis Crick, who discovered DNA, sold for £300. Another one recently came up for sale and made £18,000. I have friends who collect everything from books about the Russian royal family to children's pop-ups and from modern first editions (relatively inexpensive if you buy when first published) to nineteenth-century travel books. All offer potential for growth. For my own part I am most interested in twentieth-century Irish literature. Many of these authors are still alive (prices tend to increase when an author dies), and although the biggest names, such as W. B. Yeats and Samuel Beckett (we are now celebrating his centenary), are out of my league, a host of others—including Seamus Heaney, William Trevor, Molly Keane, Brian Moore, Flann O'Brien and the late John McGahern—are still available at reasonable prices.

One final question that needs to be answered is where to buy. I would not, on the whole, recommend the internet. Sites such as Abe Books (www.abebooks.com), which offers more than 70 million volumes from 13,000 dealers and sells more than 20,000 books a day, are not for the inexperienced. Books are frequently described inaccurately and overvalued. Far better to buy at auction (all the major auction houses hold regular sales) or through a reputable dealer. If you are interested in Irish books, by the way, I suggest a visit to Cathach Books (10 Duke Street, Dublin 2; www.rarebooks.ie), which has a well-earned reputation for providing honest, friendly advice. Incidentally, once you know what you are looking for you may be surprised by how much you can pick up in ordinary second-hand bookshops, charity shops and even privately.

(First published 3 December 2006)

10 | ALL TOGETHER NOW
DEBT CONSOLIDATION

If you are interested in making money there is one simple but incredibly effective step you can take to dramatically increase your wealth. It's a step that, for a typical family, could mean as much as €100 to €2,000 or even more, tax-free, to spend or save every month.

Interested? All it involves is reviewing your loans—mortgage, bank borrowing, leasing, credit cards and other debts—and reorganising them so that you pay the lowest amount of interest and repayment. This may not sound a very worthwhile activity, so let me start with a real-life example involving two of my clients, who I will call, in order to preserve their confidentiality, Adrian and Carmel O'Sullivan.

The O'Sullivans are in a good financial position, with two incomes and plenty of equity in their home. When they came to speak to me their borrowings were as follows:

Type of loan	Remaining term	Rate	Amount	Monthly cost
Mortgage	18 years (25-year term)	4.03%	€234,000	€1,239.02
Home improvement	4 years (5-year term)	8.5%	€18,000	€369.30
Car loan	2 years (4-year term)	7.5%	€20,000	€483.58
Credit card 1	n.a.	16.9%	€6,000	€300.00
Credit card 2	n.a.	10%	€4,000	€200.00
Store card	n.a.	23%	€8,000	€400.00

Although they could well afford the total cost of their loan repayments—€2,991.90 a month—they were paying much more than they needed to for their borrowing. I suggested that they consolidate—in other words, move all their debt (€290,000) to a single lender—and thus benefit from a considerably lower rate of interest. In fact, as they own their own home I was able to find them a new mortgage at just 3½% a year—1% over the European Central Bank rate. This gave the O'Sullivans two choices. They could carry on paying the same amount each month: the advantage of this would be that their mortgage (and all their other debts) would be paid off sooner—in just under ten years—and also that they would save a staggering €115,217 in interest; or they could take advantage of the lower interest rate I had negotiated for them to cut their monthly payments to just €1,451.81—a reduction of €1,540.09! However, if they decided to go for an interest-only loan (repaying the full amount at the end of the term or by lump sum reductions at no penalty costs during the term) their repayment at the same interest rate would be even cheaper, down to just €845.83 per month!

The O'Sullivans went for the €1,451.81 monthly payment and decided to invest the difference. As a result, from a bond investment they are looking forward to receiving a lump sum in excess of €180,000 the same year they pay their mortgage off. Their investment choices are now limitless.

Should you be following the O'Sullivans' example and thinking of consolidating your debt? If you have a variety of loans at different rates then it could save you a great deal of money. However, consolidating loans with your mortgage should be a once-in-a-lifetime strategy. This is because what you are doing is converting short-term, expensive debt to long-term, inexpensive debt. If you repeat the process then what you will gain in lower interest rates you will lose in a longer repayment term.

Consolidation requires discipline too. You'll be no better off if you replace one set of high-interest loans with another, or if you don't use your monthly saving to good purpose.

Whether or not you consolidate, it goes without saying that you should review your level of indebtedness regularly. In particular, you should

- check that you have the most competitive mortgage rate available. If you save just 0.5% a year over the term of a 25-year €250,000 home loan, it will be worth a staggering €20,409 to you.
- avoid borrowing money on credit cards or store cards. I have seen interest rates as high as 23%. If you use 'plastic', pay the balance off each month and don't fall into the 'minimum payment' trap. If you make the minimum monthly payment on a €1,000 balance at 17% it will take you eleven years to pay off the debt and cost you a staggering €1,870 in interest alone.
- never borrow to pay for living expenses or 'life-style'.

If you don't want to consolidate using a mortgage, but you

do want to reduce your debts, then you can adopt what I call the 'sniper' approach. This involves picking off your debts one at a time, starting with the most expensive. At the same time you should move your borrowing to where it will cost you least.

Attitudes to debt have changed considerably over the last few decades. Greater wealth, greater competition in the financial services sector and a period of stable, relatively low interest rates have all resulted in an explosion in consumer borrowing. This in itself is no bad thing. It makes excellent sense to borrow money for such purposes as buying a home, funding an education or making a major purchase or investment. It may also make excellent sense to borrow money and re-invest at a higher return. This column is all about making money. One of the best ways to do this is to make sure you aren't wasting your cash on expensive or unnecessary debt. If you want assistance in this area then you should consult your professional financial adviser.

(First published 7 May 2006)

11 | **IN THE CLUB**
INVESTMENT CLUBS

Have you always wanted to enjoy the sort of profit opportunities that are only possible from stock-market investment—where the annual average gain has been 17.4% from the period 1974 up to this year—but been put off by either the complexity or the cost? Or maybe you are already a shareholder and are keen to reduce your risks and increase your returns? Either way, you should consider becoming involved with an investment club.

The investment club concept is simplicity itself. A group of friends, colleagues or neighbours pool their money in order to invest in stocks and shares. To get the club started, members put in a lump sum—perhaps a few hundred euros—after which they each make a fixed monthly contribution. Some clubs call for as little as €100 a month investment, others set the limit somewhat higher. Once the club has sufficient funds it will start to make investments. At any point individual members may withdraw their cash, and a collective decision can always be made to wind the club up.

As a way of making money, investment clubs offer some fantastic benefits.

To begin with, they overcome one of the biggest problems facing private investors: how to diversify. The best way to avoid losses and optimise profits when investing is to put your money into a portfolio (or range) of different company shares. There is no magic number of companies you should invest in, but I would have said the absolute minimum was fifteen. Because of the cost of buying and selling shares it is rarely worth investing less than €2,000 in any one company, so for a private investor to even begin to diversify he or she must have at least €30,000—and ideally considerably more. This is a lot of money for many individuals to find, but not for an investment club. For instance, a club with twenty members contributing €300 each on day 1 and €25 a week thereafter would manage it in under a year.

The next advantage that investor clubs offer is that the members are pooling more than their money. Deciding which company shares to buy in order to maximise your returns is a time-consuming business. First you have to select the sectors you are interested in. Then you have to pick out companies you believe will do best. Given that more than seventy companies are listed on the Irish Stock Exchange, 2,800 on the London Stock Exchange and 6,784 on the various American stock exchanges (not to mention all the other stock markets around the world), it is definitely a case of 'many hands make light work.' Furthermore, different members of the club may have specialist industry knowledge that can further boost the chances of success.

This leads to another reason for the popularity of investment clubs. They are an ideal way for novice investors to learn about stock-market investment quickly and without the worry of making costly mistakes. Speaking of costs, investor clubs are the least expensive way for a private investor to enjoy share ownership. This is partly because it is almost impossible to buy a worthwhile number of shares when you are purchasing them month by month, and partly because all the costs associated with buying and selling shares will be divided among the club members. What's more, as club members donate their time and expertise free, there should be no other expenses, such as management fees.

The first investment club was founded in Texas as long ago as 1898, and since then hundreds of thousands of clubs have been established around the world. Here in Ireland, where a lower percentage of the population own shares than in many developed countries, investment clubs were relatively rare until quite recently. Over the last few years, however, they have become increasingly popular, with new clubs being started every week.

Recognising this trend, the Irish Stock Exchange has published a booklet, *Investment Clubs: A Guide to Establishing and Running a Club for Equity Investors in Ireland*. This excellent free guide not only explains how investor clubs work but includes an invaluable section on managing club finances, stockbroking services, record-keeping, and tax issues. Most useful of all, it includes all the legal documents you will need, including sample rules, meeting agendas and constitution. You can download the entire booklet of twenty pages from the ISE web site (www.ise.ie), or write to the Irish Stock Exchange, 28 Anglesey Street, Dublin 2.

Incidentally, there are various companies trying to cash in on the growing popularity of investment clubs. These are generally trying to sell seminars, software, financial advice or stockbroking services and, in some cases where no expertise exists within your club, may well be of benefit to the members. There are only two non-profit investment club organisations offering free, worthwhile advice. These are Pro-share in Britain (www.proshareclubs.co.uk) and the National Association of Investors Corporation in the United States (www.betterinvesting.org). Both can furnish information and case histories. The latter is especially encouraging, as many investment clubs achieve well above average returns.

Although the main reason for establishing an investment club is to make money, there is another advantage that shouldn't be overlooked. Being part of a club is extremely enjoyable. While meetings may have a serious purpose, they are often informative and entertaining.

Before making any financial decision you should always take professional advice.

(First published 14 May 2006)

12 | **GRAPE EXPECTATIONS**
VINTAGE WINES

Can you guess how much twelve bottles of Le Pin 1982, which cost €280 the year it was released, are worth today? The answer is €35,000. That's a gain of more than 12,000% in twenty-four years.

Naturally, not all wine investments perform as well; but over the short, medium and long term a well-chosen portfolio of wine should produce excellent returns. In 2005 Live-ex.com, a stock exchange for the wine industry, grew by 18.7%. During the last decade Decanter.com, another index that measures market performance, has shown an average annual return of 20%. Peter Foley of the industry experts Berry Brothers and Rudd (www.bbr.com) states that over the longer term 15% profit a year is feasible. Profit is not the only reason why wine makes such an attractive investment. Even if you aren't an *oenophile* (for all you pint drinkers, that's a connoisseur of fine wines) it is a fascinating subject to study. What's more, if your investment fails to make you money, you can always drink it.

The first step to investing in wine is to understand the market. The best wines mature once they have been bottled and carry on improving with age. Every year the greatest producers can only create a finite supply. As that supply is consumed, so availability becomes limited and prices begin to rise. To maximise your gains you may choose to buy your wine *en primeur*—in the summer after the harvest and a full eighteen months before it will be bottled. The safest and most secure investment option is to buy French wine; the top performers historically have always been the leading thirty châteaux in Bordeaux. Some Spanish and even New World wines could well appreciate—but the risk is substantially higher.

It is worth remembering that how much a wine costs is not automatically an indicator of its quality. Fashion often pushes prices up. In the 1960s, for instance, German Liebfraumilch became popular and prices rose. Mass production and poor quality control meant that these gains were short-lived.

The most influential wine commentator in the world is almost certainly an American called Robert Parker. Recently he described the 2005 Bordeaux vintage as 'the finest vintage in memory.' It will shortly be available *en primeur*, and it is likely that long before it is released in 2008 the price will have risen by as much as 100% to 150% or even more. Not everyone believes that a well-trained palate such as Parker's is required to spot a potential winner. Orley Ashenfelter, an economist at Princeton University, has analysed the market, going back many years, and has found that the average temperature during the growing season, rainfall in August and September and rainfall the previous winter are actually the essential factors in determining price. On this basis the 2005 vintage, which could cost anything up to £3,000 a case *en primeur*, may not produce such large gains as other vintages.

Disagreements over the investment potential for any

particular wine illustrate the need for expert advice. Experienced buyers may choose to purchase at auction, but for anyone else it is more sensible to purchase through a wine merchant. You can check whether a wine merchant is reputable, incidentally, by visiting www.investdrinks.org, and you can check prices by signing up for the professional version of www.wine-searcher.com. Your merchant can also arrange storage for you. This must be in a temperature-controlled warehouse. When you come to sell your investment it will be worth considerably less if you don't possess documentary evidence to prove it has been stored properly. Thanks to the creation of the euro zone, by the way, it may make more sense to buy and store your wine in France, where both supply and demand are stronger than here in Ireland.

If you are attracted by the idea of investing in wine you may like to bear in mind the following tips:

- It is possible to buy wine without having to pay duty or VAT until such time as you either take delivery or sell the wine on. This is called buying 'in bond', and your wine will be kept in a 'bonded warehouse'. Clearly, this saving will maximise your gains.
- Buy complete cases (never mixed cases). A case will be more valuable if it is of the original wood and unopened. If you can afford it, buy more than one case of the same wine, as this is what purchasers are often looking for. You shouldn't automatically buy just the famous names: there could be more profitable investments to be made.
- Don't economise on insurance. Make sure that your wine is covered at the market price and not just the price you paid for it.
- Make sure you know the provenance and storage history of any wine you buy. The trade attracts a certain

number of unscrupulous so-called investment advisers. Only deal with actual wine merchants.

- Wine is generally considered a medium to long-term investment. You probably shouldn't consider selling for at least five years.

Wine is an alternative investment. For this reason you should only consider it if you have already bought property, equities and bonds. Under such circumstances, however, it is not unreasonable to have grape expectations.

(First published 21 May 2006)

13 | ALL YOURS
FRANCHISING

How would you like to receive a regular income (and enjoy the prospect of a capital gain) from your own successful company? Nowadays owning a lucrative business doesn't necessarily mean being highly entrepreneurial, making a huge investment or taking much risk. Because, thanks to franchising, it is possible to buy a turnkey business concept with a proven record and almost guaranteed profits. What's more, with close to two hundred established franchise options in Ireland you have plenty of choice. You could, for instance, invest your cash in a business and employ a management team to run it for you; buy a business with the help of a loan and work in it yourself; or effect a combination of the two. Whichever route you choose, franchising offers some incredible moneymaking opportunities.

Although franchising has really only taken off in Ireland over the last decade, its history can be traced back to America in the 1850s, when the Singer Sewing Machine Company appointed franchisees to distribute its products. Over the space of 150 years the basic principle hasn't altered much. In exchange for an initial payment, a franchisee gains a number of privileges, which may include the rights to

- sell a particular product or service,
- use a set of business practices based on the parent company's experience in the field,
- receive initial training, and
- benefit from an assortment of continuing support services, such as advertising and accounts.

As the parent company—known as the *franchisor*—will receive a percentage of the gross sales, it is in its interest to ensure that the franchisee is successful. To this end a good franchisor will invest huge sums of money in making certain that its business formula is as effective as possible. From the location of the business to the quality of the customer service, nothing will be left to chance. It is this factor that takes much of the risk out of setting up a franchise. Follow the rules and all the statistics show that you are much more likely to succeed with a franchise than any other type of business.

Not that franchises suit everyone. True, you will be purchasing a tried and tested business concept, benefiting from an established trade name and receiving all the information and support you need to get started quickly and easily. Against this you should bear in mind that your franchise agreement will contain all sorts of restrictions. You won't be able to initiate anything new or introduce innovations. Furthermore, you will be dependent on the franchisor's reputation, you may be forced to buy the franchisor's products at an inflated price and you won't be able to sell the business on without the franchisor's approval.

All franchisors are not equal either. While new franchisors will charge you less, they have less of a reputation and less at stake if things don't work out for you. Big, internationally known franchisors, on the other hand, won't want to risk damaging their brand with a business failure.

As there are franchises covering every conceivable sector, from fast food to business consultancy and from office cleaning to printing, it is important to choose an area that interests you. No business owner can expect to succeed if he or she isn't passionate about what they are doing. Another consideration will be your budget. Larger franchises, such as McDonald's or Statoil, require substantial six-figure (and even seven-figure) investments. However, you can purchase a more modest franchise—such as the Stretch-n-Grow children's fitness programme or Oscar's pet food delivery service—for about the price of a new car. Generally speaking, the more you invest the lower the risk and the easier it will be to employ someone to run the business for you.

If you had wanted to buy a franchise in Ireland a decade ago you might have struggled to find support and financing. Over the last couple of years, however, franchising has come into its own. All the major banks have specialist advisers and information on the subject. All are keen to lend. There are innumerable organisations offering information too, including the following:

Irish Franchise Association
30 Tolka Valley Business Park
Dublin 11
Phone: (01) 4991091
Web site: www.irishfranchiseassociation.com

International Franchise Association
1350 New York Avenue NW
Suite 900
Washington, DC 20005-4709

USA
Phone: 00 1 202 6288000
Web site: www.franchise.org

British Franchise Association
Franchise Chambers
Thames View
Newton Road
Henley-on-Thames, Oxfordshire RG9 1HG
England
Phone: 00 44 1491 578050
Web site: www.british-franchise.org

I would also recommend a number of web sites, including www.whichfranchise.ie, www.franchisesolutions.com and www.franchisedirect.com. Finally, before taking any major financial decision you would be well advised to talk to your financial adviser. A competent financial adviser will be able to negotiate better terms (and lower rates) with a lender than you will be able to negotiate yourself.

(First published 28 May 2006)

14 | **ALMOST FAMOUS**
ROCK AND POP
MEMORABILIA

It may only be rock and roll, but investors love it. During the last few days of May, while stock markets all around the world were suffering from a mild attack of the jitters, two international auction houses, Christie's and Bonham's, achieved (no pun intended) record prices for some of the choicest rock and pop memorabilia ever offered.

There can be no doubt that buying a shirt that once belonged to John Lennon or a concert programme signed and inscribed by Elvis Presley to Elton John's mother is infinitely riskier than investing in stocks and shares. Nevertheless, the market's appetite for any item directly connected to the biggest names in music entertainment of the last fifty years appears to be insatiable, making it a good option for anyone with a little cash to spare and a desire to earn above-average returns.

Rock and pop memorabilia meet all the requirements for a sensible alternative investment, that is to say, the scarcity value of the objects in question is assured; demand is strong; prices have been rising steadily; and there are plenty of ways to buy and sell. Add to this the fact that there are a surprising number of serious collectors willing to spend €100,000 or more for top items and you will understand why investors have been diversifying into everything from Michael Jackson's sequined gloves to Eric Clapton's Brownie guitar (you know, the 1956 Fender Strat he played when he was in Derek and the Dominos . . . Layla et al.).

Interestingly, the first auction of rock memorabilia was in 1970 as a fund-raiser for anti-war politicians and it raised a mere $15,000. Bargains abounded. Roger Daltrey gave a jacket he had worn at the Isle of Wight Festival and it fetched just $330; Joni Mitchell donated all the handwritten lyrics for her debut album, *Blue*, and they made just $90. Prices remained relatively low for the following decade, but in 1981 Sotheby's decided to launch a regular sale. That year they sold Paul McCartney's childhood piano for $16,920— not much when you consider that the piano John Lennon used to write 'Imagine' made $2.1 million in 1991, or that in 1996 a Canadian businessman paid a staggering $2.3 million for Lennon's psychedelic 1965 Rolls-Royce Phantom v.

As almost every item of rock or pop memorabilia is unique, it is hard to know quite how much prices have increased. Still, it is possible to make some comparisons. In 2000 a pair of John Lennon's orange-tinted sunglasses sold at auction for £7,800. In 2005 a nearly identical pair made £63,250. That's a gain of more than 800% in just five years. Handwritten lyrics by John Lennon made £31,000 at auction in 1996. In 2005 a similar sheet of lyrics went for £690,000. That's a gain of more than 2,200% in less than a decade.

Not that you need to invest such large sums. There are plenty of worthwhile options, from a few hundred euros and above. Recently I spotted an Isle of Wight Festival poster from 1969 for €150, a pair of Elton John's platform boots for €400, and a Buddy Holly signed souvenir programme of his group's only British tour for €1,000.

Items of value divide into various categories, including gold and platinum records, acetates (vinyl records), awards, instruments, documents, clothing, autographs, photographs, promotional material (such as back-stage passes), recordings and personal property. In general, something connected to an artist's career will be worth more than a personal item. In every category, items will be valued according to a whole set of different criteria, and before you invest a penny you should familiarise yourself with what makes one thing worth more than another. Here are a few tips:

- Gold and platinum record awards were given out by the Recording Industry Association of America from 1958 onwards. As framed awards were given not just to the artists but to everyone involved in the production process, there are tens of thousands of awards in existence. The most valuable will always be those given to artists for their best-known work, and early awards, which are rarer and were framed by a white linen matte.
- Signed musical instruments are only of real value if the artist actually used them for any length of time. The value increases if the instrument was used to perform or compose a famous song and if photographic evidence exists. Also, you need to consider the intrinsic value of the instrument. A 1959 Gibson Les Paul guitar could make €100,000 at auction even if it had never been owned by someone famous.
- Lyrics have achieved some of the best prices at auction. Working lyrics will always be worth more than lyrics handwritten by the artist after a song became famous (which many artists will do for family, friends and fans). Least valuable are signed copies of printed lyrics.
- Legal documents—such as contracts—may or may not

be valuable, depending on who the artist is and what the contract concerned. Note that many people are fooled into believing they have found a copy of the Who's original Woodstock contract when in fact they have a facsimile from their 1970 album *The Who Live at Leeds*.

- Autographs are widely collected and, as a result, widely forged.
- The most desirable costumes and clothes are those worn by the most famous artists on stage at well-known events, in music videos for hit songs or during publicity photo shoots. Not very long ago the denim vest worn by Madonna in a promotional shoot went for $25,000.

As with any alternative investment, you should only buy objects that you will enjoy owning whether the value goes up or down. You should always buy from reputable auction houses and dealers; Christie's, Sotheby's and Bonham's all hold regular sales, and other specialists worth contacting are Cooper Owen (www.cooperowen.com), It's Only Rock and Roll (www.itsonlyrocknroll.com), and Julien's Auctions (www.juliensauctions.com). There are lots of books on the subject, but my favourite is the lavishly illustrated *Christie's Rock and Pop Memorabilia*.

I must confess to being passionately interested in this area. Not only am I part of a little six-piece band—music is also in the blood—but I have various items myself, including one of the only twenty-five Lee denim jackets made for the Jerry Lee Lewis biopic *Great Balls of Fire*. Recently it was valued at $5,000. The jacket was actually a present nearly ten years ago, but that jacket represents an ever-increasing asset, and, needless to say, it's framed.

(First published 11 June 2006)

15 | READY WHEN YOU ARE
BUILDING UP A RAINY-DAY FUND

Would you like to have plenty of spare cash—sitting in a convenient bank account—for when you need it? I am talking about a bank account with sufficient funds to ensure that you can pay for unexpected expenses, extra purchases or emergencies without having to think twice? A bank account, for that matter, that you could use to take advantage of any hot investment opportunities that come your way?

One of the most important methods of ensuring your long-term financial welfare is to create a cash reserve. Not only will it serve as a safety net but it will also speed up the whole process of building up your wealth. Without a cash reserve you will always be vulnerable to

- large, irregular bills—such as maintenance on your home or car
- any fall in your income—whether due to illness, unemployment or some other reason
- any increase in expenses—perhaps because the cost of borrowing has gone up.

With a cash reserve, on the other hand, you will be financially invincible. You won't have to borrow unnecessarily (which could be a huge drain on your future income) and—once your cash reserve reaches an appropriate level—you will free up money for more lucrative investment purposes.

What is an appropriate level for a cash reserve? This will depend on your personal circumstances. If you are single and in your twenties or early thirties, with low overheads and no responsibilities, for instance, then you probably only need enough cash to cover, say, three months' worth of expenditure. On the other hand, if you are married with children, a mortgage and a car to run you should probably aim to build up as much as six months' expenditure.

If you don't have a lump sum available to put into your cash reserve then the best thing to do is to establish a pattern of regular saving each week or each month. Remember, something is better than nothing: even if it is a relatively small amount it will soon add up. Saving this way is something many people mean to do but just never get around to. Here are some tips to help you:

- Saving can only be achieved by conscious effort. You have to make a decision to save regularly and then put your plan into action.
- You should open a savings account somewhere convenient (I'll make some suggestions in a moment) and arrange to make regular payments into it.
- One of the best ways of saving money is to set up a standing order from your current account into your savings account (e.g. ssia).
- Your employer may have a 'payroll deduction' scheme, which could be worth investigating.
- If you have any extra income, for instance child allowance from the state, you could consider saving all

of this on an automatic basis.

- Before you begin, decide under what circumstances you will use your savings and don't touch them for any other reason. Your savings should be sacrosanct.

Incidentally, if you are in a permanent relationship then ideally you should both have access to your cash reserve. If something happens to one of you, then the other may need to use this money.

When deciding where to build up and keep your cash reserve, there are three things to consider.

1. **The level of interest you will be receiving.** It is well worth shopping around, as rates vary enormously. At the moment some of the best rates are available from telephone-only, internet-only or telephone-and-internet-only accounts, for example Rabobank (www.rabodirect.ie), which is offering 3.35%, and Northern Rock (www.northernrock-ireland.ie), which is offering 3.45%. Anglo-Irish Bank PLC—with a physical branch and broker presence—offers 3% interest on a thirty-day notice account as well as 4.5% for a two-year regular saving account of between €100 and €1,000 per month. These compare very well when you consider that some financial institutions pay as little as 0.1% on deposit and 0% on current accounts.

2. **The level of access you have.** You must be able to get your money easily when you need it. Many financial institutions, however, will offer you a higher return if you agree to give them notice when you plan to make a withdrawal, for instance if you give them thirty days' notice or even ninety days' notice. They will charge you a penalty if you don't provide such notice, which could wipe out any interest you have earned. One idea is to keep some of your savings in an 'instant access' account and the rest in a 'notice account'.

3. **The amount of tax you will have to pay.** The only tax-

free options available are from An Post. You could consider, for example, its instalment savings scheme, which offers a competitive, tax-free return. Once you have a lump sum, An Post savings certificates may also be appropriate. Otherwise the government will automatically claim deposit interest retention tax (DIRT) at 20% on your interest. If you are a higher-rate taxpayer you may also have to pay PRSI. However, if you are not liable for income tax, if you or your spouse is over sixty-five years of age or you are permanently incapacitated then you are entitled to claim back DIRT. What's more, you can make a back claim for DIRT tax for up to six years. To reclaim DIRT ask for a form from any larger post office, bank, building society or tax office.

Banks and building societies are, of course, the obvious place to build up a cash reserve. However, don't forget the benefits offered by membership of a credit union. The interest rate offered is always higher than ordinary bank deposit accounts and their opening hours more practical for their customers.

(First published 18 June 2006)

16 POOL PARTY

MANAGED FUNDS/POOLED INVESTMENTS

Are you looking for an investment that could earn you a very decent return without undue risk? I'm talking of an average gain—in the present climate— of around 15% a year or more.

Whether you have a lump sum to invest or want to save regularly, one of the best options open to you is to pool your money with other investors in a managed fund. Managed funds, which include *pooled investments, unit trusts* and *investment trusts*, come in all shapes and sizes but share one important benefit: they allow you to diversify.

Diversification is vital if you want to build your wealth safely and steadily. Instead of putting your money somewhere secure but unprofitable—or risking losses in an attempt to make it grow faster—you invest it in more than one area. In doing this you are able to balance risk and reward.

If you have plenty of capital—ideally hundreds of thousands of euros—diversification can be achieved directly by buying a range of shares, starting a pension fund, purchasing property and so forth. If your resources are more limited, however, the same effect can be obtained by buying units in a managed fund.

With any managed fund, your money—along with the money of all the other participants—is pooled and then invested. Each fund will have its own objectives or aims. For example, one might invest in energy companies, another in large Irish companies, a third in European property. The advantages offered by managed funds include:

- You can invest in areas that would otherwise be closed to smaller, private investors. Imagine how rich you would have to be to buy shares in, say, fifty different oil, gas and power companies or to actually purchase dozens of giant office blocks around the world.
- You will get the benefit of expert advice. The managers of each fund are professional investment specialists. Together with their researchers and analysts, they will seek out the best profit opportunities on your behalf.
- You can choose funds that meet your needs. Some are designed for growth, while others are designed to pay you an income.
- You can start investing with as little as €50 a month or a €5,000 lump sum.
- Although these types of investment should be considered as medium-term (a minimum of five years) to long-term, you always have access to your money if you need it. This differs from many direct investments, where you have to wait to find a buyer.

How do managed funds actually work? When you invest your money—whether it is a lump sum or a monthly payment—you will be allocated units in the fund. Each unit has a value linked to the underlying value of the fund's investments. In simplistic terms, if a fund consisted of €100,000,000 of investments and there were 10,000,000 units, each unit would be worth €10. If the fund's investments rose in value by 10%, then each unit would rise by 10%—making them worth €11 each. In fact there is a very slight difference between the cost of buying a unit and the value you receive when you sell it. These two prices are expressed as *bid* and *offer*, and the difference is the *spread*.

The financial institutions running managed funds expect to get paid for their expertise.

- Virtually all funds charge an entry fee of up to 5% of the amount you are investing.
- There will definitely be an annual management fee—usually 1% of the amount invested.
- You may also be charged a fee when you want to sell units.

Some people become obsessed with the charges made by managed funds. To my mind this is irrelevant. What really counts is the performance. If a fund manager is producing good returns, what does it matter of they are charging you 0.85% or 0.93% a year?

Choosing a managed fund is no different from making any other investment decision. The first step is to decide what your financial objectives are. How long do you want to invest the money for? How much risk do you want to take? What sort of returns do you want to achieve? Is there any particular investment area that interests you?

The next step is to draw up a short list of possible managed funds. There are more than 1,631 funds available in Ireland and you will find details of them in the *Irish Independent* on Thursday, the *Irish Times* on Friday, the *Sunday Times* and the *Sunday Business Post* or if you visit any of the investment or insurance companies' own web sites, such as New Ireland/Bank of Ireland's investment web site, www.Smartfunds.ie.

When considering different managed funds it is important to remember that—

- over the long term the stock market has performed better than any other investment option
- the best way to invest in the stock market is to buy units in a general managed fund, unit trust, indexed fund or stock market 'basket'
- past performance is no guide to future performance. Just because a fund did well last year—or for the last ten or twenty years—doesn't mean it will automatically do well in the future
- fund managers move around. It can be worth noting the names of successful managers and watching to see when they move to a new or different fund.

Over the last twelve months the average Irish managed fund rose 15.6% and the average annual return over the last three years is 14.6%. When I asked Thomas Hughes, who is the head of life and pensions in Providence Finance, for some specific recommendations he insisted that it would depend on the investor's circumstances. However, he personally likes the look of Canada Life's Dividend Bond, which has produced 86.8% return up to 31 March 2006 since its inception (10 March 2003), New Ireland's Evergreen Fund (the longest-running managed fund in Ireland), which has produced a solid 10.3% per year annualised return over the last three years and has never fallen over any five-year period since it was founded in 1971, and New Ireland's High Yield Equity Fund, which is a relatively new fund and has produced, up to 8 June 2006, a 57.6% return since inception (18 September 2003).

You should always take independent professional financial advice before making any investment.

(First published 25 June 2006)

17 | CASHING IN ON A CRASH
BUYING IN AT THE
BOTTOM OF A CYCLE

Are you interested in arranging your finances so that whatever happens to the economy you carry on making money? Share prices and property prices may fall, inflation and interest rates may rise, but there is no reason why—with a bit of careful planning—you shouldn't turn every situation to your advantage. In fact if you are ready for it a recession could be a once-in-a-lifetime opportunity to fast-track your wealth.

Before I explain how you can cash in on any future downturn let me just say that I am not predicting a doom-and-gloom scenario any time soon. After their meeting in St Petersburg in early June, finance ministers from the Group of Eight countries released a joint statement in which they said that 'global growth remains strong and is gradually becoming more broad-based.' Here in Ireland there is certainly every reason to believe that the economy is in robust shape. Nevertheless, it is always prudent to be prepared. After all, markets move in cycles, and sooner or later the current cycle must or at least may come to an end. Furthermore, a little advance planning won't cost you a penny and could well earn you a fortune.

If you want to profit from a slump—or even a small slip—there are three different steps you need to follow.

Firstly, you must make sure that your existing assets are recession-proof.

After all, there is no point in making money in one area only to be losing it in another. Many of the world's most successful investors follow a strategy of cashing in on gains long before they believe the market has reached the top of the cycle. In this way they optimise their returns without suffering unnecessary losses.

Whether you follow this course or not, one thing you must do is diversify. Don't imagine that because, say, you own a basket of shares in blue-chip multinationals in different parts of the world you have reduced your exposure to risk. In recent weeks we have seen that a geographical spread of leading equity markets has offered little protection.

Instead you should invest in a broad range of assets: everything from a pension to overseas property and from managed funds to fine art.

Secondly, review your debt situation. In the present low-interest climate it has been relatively easy to borrow money, invest it, and achieve a sufficiently high return to cover the interest costs and still make a substantial profit. While no-one is predicting a return to the high interest rates of the 1980s and 90s, it is wise to consider how you would be affected by even a modest increase. Other events that might affect your net worth will depend on what assets you have. There is no magic formula that can be applied here, but for some it may make sense to use the low-interest climate to rid themselves of potentially expensive debt.

Thirdly, you want to ensure that you have sufficient cash or liquid assets on hand to seize opportunities when they arise. On 11 June the business section of this newspaper asked leading Irish business chiefs whether the recent dip in the stock market was the beginning of a major and sustained crash in the stock markets or just a small correction. The most interesting answer, to my mind, came from Tom McAleese, managing director of Barclays Ireland, who pointed out that every price fall was a buying opportunity. A fall in the stock market of 10%—which is what the world has experienced recently—means that shares are now worth 10% less than they were a few months ago. Given that companies are reporting strong earnings, valuations are in effect lower: profits have gone up but share prices have not. If and when we enter a bear market it is the investors who have cash available who will clean up. They will be able to buy into solid, asset-backed companies at bargain basement prices and benefit from the next upward swing.

Incidentally, what applies to a fall in the stock market applies to a fall in any other market. A general downturn in the economy will make it cheaper to buy all sorts of other valuable assets, including property and alternative assets, such as classic cars, jewellery and fine art.

Whether or not you expect even a mild recession, there is much to be said for switching out of higher-risk, higher-return assets into relatively liquid investments that can be converted to cash when a market opportunity presents itself. Gold (as I explained in an earlier article) is one place where you might put your cash. Another, perhaps more sensible option is to buy index-linked government bonds. The huge advantage offered by index-linked government bonds is that your return is certain and you are protected against a market crash, rising interest rates or inflation. Swiss bonds are widely favoured as the ultimate in security. However, a Swiss ten-year bond offers a yield of just 2.7%.

Instead, consider putting your cash into Norwegian bonds, which at present produce yields of more than 4% and— thanks to the country's oil revenues and political stability—must be considered just as safe.

(First published 2 July 2006)

18 | VA VA VOOM
CLASSIC CARS

If you are looking for an asset that is going to provide you with a great deal of enjoyment, some juicy tax savings and—crucially—the potential of a substantial capital gain, then it is hard to beat the benefits offered by investing in a classic car.

Classic cars have been showing a steady increase in value, for two reasons. Firstly, like rock memorabilia or watches, they are in sufficient demand to have gained acceptance by auction houses and other sellers keen for new business. While not exactly a liquid asset, there are plenty of ways to buy and sell a classic car, quickly and inexpensively.

Secondly, but perhaps more importantly, this demand is not limited to a select few. In the two major classic car markets—Europe and the United States—there is no shortage of affluent buyers who grew up in an era when the car defined the culture. They may not have been able to afford the car of their dreams in the 1950s, 60s or 70s, but they can certainly afford it now. This has led to some staggeringly high auction prices for the more collectable cars. Earlier this year Barrett-Jackson, an American auctioneer, sold six cars for over a million dollars each in a single month. And, thanks to the trickle-down effect, classic cars of all models and makes have been enjoying healthy price increases. Four or five years ago you could have bought an Aston Martin DB4GT for €180,000. Today the same car would fetch double the price. Not that you need to be super-rich to invest in this sector. An Aston Martin V8 can still be found for under €20,000 or a Ferrari 308 GTB for under €30,000.

So, how do you choose a classic car that will bring you both pleasure and profit? Obviously you need to pick a car that you like the look of and will enjoy driving. For a car to be considered a classic it is usually at least twenty-five years old. This said, from an investment viewpoint there are cars that may be less than a decade old—such as the Dodge Viper, Jaguar XJ220 and XJR-15 or Bugatti EB-110—that are already considered future classics. So age should not be your primary consideration from an investment viewpoint. What should be your primary consideration are the different factors that make one car worth more than another. These include:

- The manufacturer. A Morris or an Austin—no matter how good—will never have the same allure to buyers as a Ferrari or a Bugatti.
- The model. A mass-produced family car will never be worth as much as something with rarity value. Even low-production cars—such as Bentleys—will vary wildly in value. A 1980s saloon can be had for €15,000, but a 1920s racer might cost you over a million euros.
- Cultural zeitgeist. The cultural status of a car can have a major effect on its value. If the car wasn't highly desirable when it was launched it is unlikely to ever become highly desirable.
- Provenance. A car with a history—for instance a car that has won an important race or been owned by

someone famous—will always be more collectable.
- Condition. The more original and better the condition, the more likely that it will appreciate.
- The price. Up to around €60,000 the market is dominated by enthusiasts rather than collectors. That is not to say that with a bit of careful research you won't be able to identify an undiscovered classic, but the more you invest the lower the risk.

Speaking of research, part of the fun of investing in a classic car is investigating all the different possibilities. There are plenty of dealers, publications and auctioneers willing to provide help. Nor should you ignore the plethora of specialist clubs, which are an invaluable source of information.

Are there any downsides? Classic cars are not passive investments. You can't tuck them away in a bank and forget about them. They need maintenance, garaging and regular servicing by a specialist to keep them in tip-top shape. Remember too that prices can fluctuate. Happily, however, the market has stabilised since the early 1990s, when the price of a Jaguar E-type fell from its record of €150,000 to €60,000.

Which cars have produced the best returns? Competition cars and high-performance cars seem to be the most secure long-term bet, with competition cars from the 1970s and 80s perhaps offering the best scope for gain at present. Other recommendations might include something like a Jaguar XK series (XK120, XK140 and XK150), which can be had for as little as €40,000, or possibly an Aston Martin DB5 for around €80,000. If you are on a tighter budget (bearing in mind the greater risk) the Audi Quattro, BMW 2002, Citroën DS, Jaguar E-type (despite its previous fall from grace) and Volvo P800 all look interesting.

A couple of final points. If you buy a car that is over thirty years old the motor tax will only cost you €42— regardless of the car's value. Furthermore, you can insure it with a classic car policy (try Axa on 1890 200016) for a fraction of the cost of a modern car. Finally, if your company car is a classic car, remember that benefit-in-kind tax could be far less than a 2006 top-of-the-range executive car.

(First published 9 July 2006)

19 | VELVET GOLDMINE
RICHES FROM RAGS

W hat every private investor dreams of is discovering a market that is poised to grow but that hasn't yet taken off. Then, and only then, is it feasible for someone with average means to buy the best-quality items at a reasonable price, safe in the knowledge that when demand reaches fever pitch they will be able to sell for a truly spectacular profit.

For instance, if you had purchased even a modest amount of first-class Irish property, shares, art or antiques fifteen or twenty years ago you would now be sitting on massive gains. And the same has been true, at different times, for dozens of other markets, from Picasso ceramics to Romanian office blocks and from Aboriginal paintings to French farmland.

Obviously, it is possible to make an above-average return in any market with astute planning and professional advice. For really big profits, however, nothing beats getting in ahead of the pack. The trouble is, of course, finding an undiscovered market that has decent growth potential but that is stable enough to ensure that you aren't exposed to undue risk.

One sector that I believe may meet the brief is that of textiles—a market that no less an authority than the *Financial Times* recently tipped as 'a collecting field waiting to happen,' which a presenter on the television programme 'Antiques Roadshow' described as 'poised for growth' and which the magazine *Forbes* predicted would 'soon enjoy increased demand from young investors looking to build their collections and decorate their homes.'

What do I mean by 'textiles'? Any man-made material, from a 3,500-year-old sheet of royal Egyptian linen to a twentieth-century tapestry, taking in medieval wall hangings and nineteenth-century Irish lace along the way. Indeed one of the attractions of textiles is that it offers such a wide range of choice. You could build up a general collection or you could specialise in Indonesian silk shawls, bark clothes with abstract designs produced by the pygmy people of the Congo, European crewel wool work hangings, samplers, Chinese sleeve bands, Aubusson tapestries, or Victorian quilts—to name just a few of the possibilities.

Generally speaking, prices have been rising slowly but steadily for several decades. However, many experts within the market feel that it is about to take off. This is because

- young collectors who can't afford to buy, say, a first-class Old Master can afford to buy the very best examples of antique textiles.
- the market is waking up to the fact that textiles are—essentially—works of art. They can be displayed with the same effect as a painting.
- supply is scarce. Many of the best pieces are in museums or historic houses like Farmleigh.
- there are plenty of undiscovered 'masterpieces' to be found. Even quite experienced antique dealers and auction houses frequently fail to recognise really valuable pieces.

- the major auction houses have been investing in their textile departments and also holding regular specialist sales, making the market more liquid.
- there is a growing number of collectors, dealers and shows specialising in textiles.

Evidence of the potential offered by investing in textiles abounds. Last month Sotheby's sold 170 items from Lord McAlpine's enormous textile collection, including twenty flags produced by the Fante people of southern Ghana about a hundred years ago. Lord McAlpine did not disclose how much he had paid for each of the flags but indicated that it was next to nothing. Most of them sold for several thousand pounds each. The buyers were probably partly drawn by the colourful, dramatic and surprisingly contemporary designs and partly by the thought that these flags may be the next 'suzanis'.

Suzanis are one category of textile that has already started to show dramatic increases in value. Suzanis are silk-on-silk or silk-on-cotton embroideries made from about 1750 to 1850 in the villages that lined the fabled Silk Road in what is now Uzbekistan. They were originally intended to be part of a bride's dowry, and their intricate, colourful designs first came to the attention of Westerners in the 1970s. Thirty years ago you might have paid as little as €20 or €30 for a fine example. Today prices start at around €3,500 and go up to €70,000 or more.

If you are interested in investing in textiles, here are some hints to get you started.

- Look for a specific area that appeals to you and learn as much about it as you can. You'll find there are plenty of books, magazines, web sites and societies to help you.
- Sotheby's, Christie's and all the other major auction houses have started to hold regular specialist sales. If

you look through recent catalogues (all available on line) you will get a good idea of prices.

- Two excellent publications to look at are *Hali* (www.hali.com) and *Textile* (www.bergpublishers. com).
- The Textile Society (www.textilesociety.org) is one of several non-profit organisations that help collectors.
- There are a number of major textile fairs every year; one where many dealers exhibit is the Hali Fair (www.halifair.com).
- Once you have decided what you are going to collect, invest in the most highly prized examples you can afford.
- Remember, you don't need a lot of cash to invest in textiles. For proof take a look at some dealers' web sites. A good example at the bottom end of the market is Meg Andrews's site (www.meg-andrews.com), where you will find fantastic examples, starting from a few hundred pounds.

I would like to stress that, unlike, say, Old Masters or fine china, there are very few people with sufficient knowledge of the textile market to recognise good pieces when they come up for sale. If you are happy to search antique shops, markets, on line and at auctions you should be able to pick up undiscovered and undervalued examples at a fraction of their true worth. A definite case of being able to turn rags into riches.

(First published 23 July 2006)

20 | **HARD TO LICK**
PHILATELY—STAMP COLLECTING

If you think of stamp-collecting as a pointless, unexciting—even dull—hobby then it is time to think again. Quietly, as befits such a sedentary pursuit, philately has emerged as one of the hottest and most fashionable pastimes in the world. Postage stamps are the third-largest category traded on eBay, and it is estimated that more than 30 million people now count themselves as active collectors. Much more to the point, stamps have proved to be an excellent medium to long-term investment, with average returns not so dissimilar to property or stocks and shares.

Relative to weight, stamps are the most valuable commodities you can buy. A well-balanced collection of stamps won't, obviously, produce an income but should provide substantial capital growth. Two market indices—the SG100 Stamp Price Index and the GB30 Rarities Index—offer tangible evidence of this. Both track average prices and have shown annual increases of closer to 9.5% over the last ten, twenty and fifty years. Furthermore, postage stamps have always fared well in times of economic uncertainty. If you study the performance charts for the last five decades you will notice that there are no dramatic market corrections. Prices may be stagnant for periods— but they rarely fall.

There are four reasons why stamps make such a sound investment. The first is growing demand. This comes from various sources, including:

- an ageing population in the developed world with the income and time to devote to a hobby such as stamp-collecting
- rapidly expanding interest in countries experiencing new levels of wealth, such as China, Russia, India and Brazil
- investors who use stamps as a hedge against risk. A good example of this was before China took over Hong Kong, when wealthy Hong Kong residents bought stamps because they were portable and valuable.

The second is, undoubtedly, the scarcity of supply, as clearly there is a limited number of any given stamp in existence. Thirdly, the market is international and liquid. This is all the more true thanks to the internet, which allows collectors to buy and sell quickly and easily. Fourthly, with astute buying it is possible for the enthusiastic philatelist to beat the market indices and produce even higher returns.

How should you set about investing in stamps? It would be unwise to start without familiarising yourself with the history of the postal service and postage stamps. You would also be well advised to understand how stamps are valued as well as how to care for them. Finally, you should consider what sort of collection you want to build up. Are you interested in stamps from a particular country, air-mail stamps, stamps that deal with a particular subject? Would you be more interested in 'covers' (where the stamp is still attached to the envelope) or unused stamps or commemorative issues?

One area of obvious interest to readers of this paper is that of collecting Irish stamps. Between 1840 (when the first of 72 million 'Penny Blacks' were printed in England) and 1922 we used British stamps, which are referred to as 'GB used in Ireland'. The most sought-after stamps for Irish collectors were the British stamps that were overprinted for Irish use, first printed in February 1922 and the last one in 1935. Between 1922 and 1984 the Department of Posts and Telegraphs had the responsibility for printing stamps, after which it passed to the newly created An Post. The 166 years of post in Ireland offer hundreds of collecting possibilities, such as the 1865–67 Fenian issue, produced by Irish veterans of the American Civil War, the banned 'propaganda labels' issued between 1907 and 1916 by Sinn Féin and, as already stated, overprinted British stamps used as a temporary measure by Rialtas Sealadach na hÉireann (Provisional Government of Ireland) in 1922.

Whatever area you decide to invest in, a stamp collection should deliver returns that are difficult to lick.

Top philately investment tips:

- If you are buying for investment purposes take specialist advice from an auction house, dealer or experienced philatelist. Some dealers, such as Stanley Gibbons (www.stanleygibbons.com), actually offer special investment products with guaranteed returns.
- Before you buy, determine your investment objectives and decide on a strategy. It is sensible to build up a diversified portfolio of stamps in the same way that you would build up a diversified portfolio of shares.
- A low-risk strategy would be to collect in a well-established, popular area—avoiding anything that might be prone to speculative influences.
- A higher-risk (and potentially higher-return) strategy would be to anticipate future demand. For instance,

you might decide to invest in stamps from an emerging country where stamp-collecting is still in its infancy.

- If you become passionate about philately then you could try to corner a new market and thus push up prices. To do this you need to find an area that is unpopular, esoteric or in some other way neglected. Build up a collection of high-quality examples at a relatively low cost, then publish a definitive guide to the subject and—hopefully—watch the prices rise.
- Always buy the best examples you can afford.
- Educate yourself about your purchases. Understand what you are buying and why it is of value.
- Remember, stamps are alternative investments. You should invest in more traditional sectors—such as the stock market and property—first. Be very aware of the risks involved and always seek professional advice.

Useful contacts

'Stampa'—the Irish National Stamp Exhibition—takes place annually in the RDS, Dublin. Annual membership costs just €25. PO Box 2723, Cardiff Lane, Dublin 2; www.stampa.ie.

The Irish Philatelic Society and the Dublin Stamp Society meet in Ely Place, Dublin (Knights of Columbanus), but no meetings during the summer. Contact Declan O'Kelly, Cathedral Stamps, Dublin; phone (01) 8786384.

Irelandstamps.com, 5 Rathgar Place, Dublin 6; phone (01) 4972520; www.irelandstamps.com.

Raven Stamps Ireland, 12C Washington Street West, Cork; phone (021) 4271750; www.irstamps.com.

(First published 30 July 2006)

21 | DO IT YOURSELF

BUILDING YOUR OWN SHARE PORTFOLIO

How feasible is it for a small private investor to build up a valuable portfolio of shares? The answer is: very. You don't need experience. You don't need to be particularly wealthy. You just need to put in a little time and patience and to follow the five straightforward steps outlined below.

Step 1: Find a stockbroker. Before you can buy (or sell) a single share you must open an account with a stockbroker. Stockbrokers charge in different ways—some on a flat fee basis, others on commission. The best rates are often to be found on line (for example www.sharewatch.com). To begin with, you may prefer to pay a bit more to a broker offering information and advice to small investors. There are stockbrokers who will make detailed suggestions and even manage your money for you—but unless you are very rich this will be too expensive. Starting out, especially if you aren't investing a lot of cash, you'll be better off making your own decisions and using an 'execution-only' service, whereby the broker literally just buys and sells on your behalf.

Step 2: Develop a strategy. The whole idea behind

building a portfolio is to buy shares in a range of different sectors so as to maximise your gains and minimise your risk. If you want to follow a relatively conservative strategy you might decide to put the majority of your money into 'defensive' and 'income' stocks, with the balance going into 'growth' stocks.

Taking stock . . . a quick guide to different types of stock

Defensive stocks are shares in companies that should continue to make profits, regardless of what is happening to the economy as a whole. Traditionally this would include health care, utilities, software and consumer staples, such as food, drink and tobacco. Examples would include IAWS Group (food and agribusiness), C&C Group (which owns Bulmers Cider) and Kerry Group (food and beverages).

Income stocks are shares in more mature businesses, which tend to pay out higher dividends (or income) to their shareholders. Income stocks often own the leading brand in their sector and have the purchasing power and market share to keep competitors at bay. Examples would include AIB (financial services), Grafton Group (retail) and Elan (pharmaceuticals).

Growth stocks are shares in companies that may pose a slightly higher risk but offer you the potential for much larger gains. Examples would include Kingspan Group (building materials), Ryanair (airlines) and Paddy Power (bookmakers).

Step 3: Search for opportunities. The most exciting part of investing directly in the stock market is choosing the individual companies to back. Perhaps the best way to start is to find products you admire and then research the companies that manufacture them. This approach will result in your looking at the world in a very different way. Everything you do or experience, from shopping to watching television and from travelling to banking, will become investment research. You may also find inspiration by observing trends and searching out companies that appear to be exploiting them successfully. For instance, with oil prices so high you may feel now is the time to invest in biotech companies. Reading newspapers and magazines will also give you ideas. When you find companies you are interested in, contact them directly for information, search the internet for further data, and don't forget to see what different brokers and analysts say about them. In general, it is better to stick to businesses and sectors you understand.

Step 4: Start buying! Dealing costs, in particular, are a big issue for small investors. However, if you are buying shares with a view to holding them over the medium to long term, dealing costs are less relevant. Opinions differ on how many individual shares a private investor should hold at any one time. Too few and you may be over-exposed to risk, too many and you may find it hard to keep track of your investments. For a balanced portfolio I would suggest holding shares in about twenty companies. How much should you put into each share? A minimum of €1,500 to €2,000. But don't despair if you haven't got €30,000 plus (20 shares × €1,500) to invest. Many successful investors spend years creating a balanced portfolio. If you bought €1,500 of shares a year over twenty years you could still end up with an extremely valuable holding.

Step 5: Time your selling. Making money from any investment is as much about knowing when to sell as it is about knowing what to buy, so you should have an exit strategy worked out before you start to build your portfolio. A good approach is to decide—in advance—an upper and lower price at which you will sell each stock you hold. In other words, if the price goes below a certain point you will sell and cut your losses and if it goes above a certain price you will sell and take your profits. Another approach is to copy Warren Buffet. He sometimes spends years considering an investment, and once he has made it he hardly ever sells; though it didn't take him long recently to give €31 billion to Bill Gates's charitable foundation.

Direct investment is not, of course, for everyone. You must have an active interest in the stock market and sufficient cash to ensure that the cost of buying and selling shares doesn't swallow up your profits. Under these circumstances, however, it can be a highly rewarding activity. Indeed many small private investors manage to match or even better overall market performance. If you had achieved this over the last year, every €1,000 you invested would be worth €1,150; and if you had achieved this over the last ten years every €1,000 you invested would be worth €2,800. Of course remember that you can have a lot of fun choosing this option, but also remember you should only invest money you can afford to lose.

Before making any financial decision you should always take professional advice.

(First published 13 August 2006)

22 | SPARKLING PROFITS
INVESTING IN DIAMONDS

Diamonds are not only a girl's best friend, they can also produce a rock-solid return. De Beers in South Africa, which controls 60% of the world's diamond production, has increased its prices five times in the last twenty-four months, but worldwide demand is still rising at 8% a year. In China alone, diamond sales are expanding at 25% a year. Nor is this growth limited to diamonds for jewellery. The vast majority of diamonds—some 80%—are used for industrial purposes, and here again prices have been rising, as demand outstrips supply.

The lure of diamonds as an alternative investment is easy to understand. Over the long term they have always more than held their value; they are easy to transport and—for those living in politically unstable regions of the world—to hide; and in countries with heavy death duties they can be passed down from generation to generation without attracting the attention of the tax man. Unlike almost any other investment, you can take pleasure from wearing them. Also, they are relatively liquid: there are dealers willing to buy and sell diamonds for cash in every big city.

Finally, if you know what you are doing it is possible to make well above average profits.

However, before you rush out and sink your savings into sparklers, a few words of warning: no-one has ever made serious money from diamonds, buying jewellery or loose stones at retail prices. Instead you need to follow these golden rules:

- The better the quality of a diamond, the greater the chance you have of profit and the easier it will be to sell. The demand for small, less good diamonds will fluctuate according to the economy. If you can't afford to invest at least €20,000—and, ideally, €40,000 or more—then your returns will be restricted.

- Learn all about the four Cs, which is how diamonds are valued:

Cut. This refers to the symmetry and proportions of the stone. The best-cut stones reflect the light in such a way as to optimise the fire and brilliance of the diamond. Diamonds are usually cut with fifty-eight facets, and a well-cut diamond will be classified as *ideal, excellent,* or *very good*. Don't touch any other type.

Colour. The best colour (unless you are buying coloured diamonds, of course: see below) is no colour at all! Diamonds are categorised from D to Z, with D representing the finest, colourless stones.

Clarity. Almost all diamonds incorporate tiny—quite natural—internal marks, known as *inclusions*. They may also have external marks, called *blemishes*. The fewer inclusions or blemishes the better the clarity. At the top end of the scale are *flawless* diamonds, and there are more than a dozen other classifications.

Carat weight. The larger the diamond, the more it weighs. Weight is measured in carats. These were originally seeds of the carob tree, which were of a consistent uniformity and so were used in ancient times to measure the weight of diamonds. One carat is now defined as 0.2 grams.

- You should only buy diamonds that have been certified by one of the recognised grading laboratories. The best-known of these are the Gemological Institute of America (GIA) and the European Gem Laboratory (EGL). Your diamond dealer should show you the appropriate certificate and you should satisfy yourself that it is genuine.
- Don't buy so-called 'blood diamonds'. These have been mined in Sierra Leone by workers kept in unimaginably bad conditions and then smuggled out of the country. Not only is it unethical to buy such a diamond but in the long term it will be worth less. Ask for something called a Kimberley process certificate—a sort of diamond passport that proves it has been mined ethically and legally.
- Watch for anything called 'clarity-enhanced'. This means that the diamond has been artificially enhanced. Bad news. Also, don't buy diamonds over the internet unless you know the dealer personally.
- If you believe diamond prices are likely to continue rising, then consider buying shares in diamond producers, such as Firestone Diamonds, River, Petra and Brazilian Diamonds.

- Subscribe to something called the Rapaport Diamond Report (www.diamonds.net), an up-to-the-minute price guide. Once you understand how diamonds are priced you may be shocked to discover just how much mark-up jewellers make! Buying diamonds for investment, you should expect to pay about 5–10% above the prices quoted in Rapaport. Bear in mind that if you buy your diamond in the EU it will be subject to VAT. If you buy it outside the EU and bring it home VAT will still be payable.
- Consider coloured or 'fancy' diamonds. These are pure diamonds that—by an accident of nature—have turned out pink, blue, green, amber or even red. They are much, much rarer than clear diamonds and therefore command a much higher price. The market for coloured diamonds has been growing as consumers begin to understand their scarcity value. Twenty years ago they cost less than clear diamonds. Now the best examples are the most expensive gemstones in the world.
- Research something called tanzanite. It isn't a precious stone, nor does it count as semi-precious. Discovered in 1967 in the foothills of Mount Kilimanjaro, the best stones are vivid violet-blue. Costing considerably less than diamonds, the price is volatile, but Tiffany's, the jewellers, use it a great deal and it could take off in the future, much in the way coloured diamonds have over the last two decades.

One other possibility is to invest in a managed fund that includes diamonds and diamond-mining shares in its portfolio. Examples would include Merrill Lynch Gold and General, Merrill Lynch World Mining and J. P. Morgan

Natural Resources; the latter has shown 50.6% growth in the year ending February 2006.

If you like the idea of making money from diamonds then there is no doubt the best strategy is to buy very high-quality stones and don't sell until one of the periodic bull markets, when prices can rise in leaps and bounds. This may, however, involve a bit of a wait. Thank heavens diamonds are for ever.

(First published 20 August 2006)

23 | BLACK GOLD
OIL OR RENEWABLE ENERGY SOURCES—AN EACH WAY BET

The end of the oil age, now only a matter of time, is going to present some fantastic money-making opportunities. There will be money to be made from oil itself as it becomes increasingly scarce; money to be made from new sources of energy; and money to be made from alternatives to oil-based products, such as plastic. If you are a private investor looking for serious medium to long-term gains it is by no means too early to start buying into companies that stand to profit as the oil starts to run out. By doing so you will have the double satisfaction of helping the planet and—as it were—helping yourself.

That oil will run out is not, of course, in doubt. The question is: when? One of the leading international experts in this field is Dr Colin Campbell, formerly head geologist with such companies as BP and Texaco, who happens to live in west Cork. In the past Campbell's predictions have proved uncannily accurate, and as a result he now advises a number of governments and multinationals on the forthcoming energy crisis. He now believes that oil production will reach a peak in 2007, after which less and less will be produced each year. Given escalating demand in developing countries, especially China and India, and the likelihood of disrupted supplies from the Middle East and Russia, this could push up prices sooner rather than later.

In fact what Campbell and many others forecast is an upward trend with a series of rises and falls along the way. This would suggest that for the foreseeable future oil shares are likely to experience further growth.

Not that all oil shares are likely to do equally well. As the oil wells start to run dry, those oil companies that don't diversify are obviously going to experience decreasing profits. Interestingly, only British Petroleum seems to take this threat seriously. Over the last decade it has invested billions in its highly profitable biofuels and alternative energy divisions, which probably accounts for the fact that BP has become one of the most popular traditional energy stocks in the world.

Renewable energy stocks are also proving popular. There are now more than a hundred renewable energy stocks being traded in the world, with a total value of €52 billion. In May the Renewable Energy Corporation in Norway raised $1.1 billion in an offering that was fifteen times oversubscribed, and shares in Renova, the leading ethanol producer, trade at a multiple of more than sixty times earnings. Lest you think, by the way, that ethanol is not a serious fuel option, it is worth noting that in Brazil the vast majority of cars already run on a 25% ethanol mix. What's more, Bill Gates has invested $84 million in building ethanol plants. Companies worth investigating in this sector include Biofuels, Renova and D1 Oils.

Although wind, wave and solar power have all been talked about as future energy sources, it is only recently that the technology has become sophisticated enough to be considered viable. Companies worth following include

Clipper Windpower, Novera, Monkton, Romag and PowerFilm. Tidal turbines are still in the early stages of development, by the way, but Ocean Power Technologies and Renewable Energy Holdings are two shares to watch.

If you are searching for other sorts of companies that stand to gain from the move to renewable energy sources you may like to consider AgCert in Dublin (involved in large-scale reduction of greenhouse gas emissions), Ceres (fuel cells that convert hydrogen to electricity) and Alkane (involved in building and operating methane plants). If you want to research renewable energy companies in general then visit the Earthscan web site (www.earthscan.co.uk) and search the Renewable Energy World suppliers database, which carries details of more than five thousand renewable energy companies.

If you prefer not to invest directly in shares but would rather buy into a managed fund, a number now specialise in alternative energy. Some, such as Ventus and Keydata Income, focus on one specific sector (in the case of these examples, wind power). Others, such as Impax, F&C Stewardship and Merrill Lynch New Energy Technology, offer more general exposure to the sector.

Oil is vital to all sorts of non-energy industries, and as its price has risen (it is seven times more expensive than it was in 1999) so chemical companies and agricultural processors have started to look to corn, vegetable oil and other raw materials to create bio-based chemicals and plastics. Biotech firms such as Biofine, Carghill, Codexis, Diversa, Dyadic International and Genencor use genetic engineering to produce superenzymes and bacteria that in turn can turn corn into plastics. Other companies are using different raw ingredients, such as paper sludge, rape oil and glucose, to create a huge range of environmentally responsible products, from carpets to paints and from solvents to disposable nappies. So far the market for bio-plastics is only worth $30 billion a year, but analysts predict that it will grow to be worth $150 billion by 2010.

The International Energy Agency says the world will need almost 60% more energy in 2030 than in 2002. We depend on oil for 90% of our transport and for food, pharmaceuticals, chemicals and the entire bedrock of modern life. Even if existing oil reserves last longer than expected, rising prices and global warming will push us towards alternative energy sources. Canny investors who take advantage of this trend can look forward to substantial profits.

Before making any financial decision you should always take professional advice.

(First published 3 September 2006)

24 YOUR WISH GRANTED
BUSINESS GRANTS

Every year millions and millions of euros are handed out to entrepreneurs and would-be entrepreneurs so that they can start or expand their businesses. This EU and government cash is available to anyone with the wit and tenacity to claim it. All you have to do is come up with a project that is eligible for a grant and you could be building your own wealth with the help of someone else's money. What counts as a suitable project? The sheer range of grants may surprise you. There is money to

- pay for research and development, including feasibility plans and consultancy
- fund advertising and marketing, including building a web site
- cover the cost of recruitment and—importantly—create employment
- help you start or expand a business
- meet the expense of staff training.

Best of all, once you have been allocated a grant the benefit is entirely yours. Let me give you just one example. I know of someone who received more than €75,000 to help him build a food-processing factory, €16,000 for a mobile refrigerated market stall, €9,000 towards consultancy fees, €8,000 towards the cost of training staff, and €3,000 towards marketing expenses. That is more than €111,000 of absolutely free money, which is helping him to get rich!

The first step is to work out realistic grant objectives. Different grants are offered for different purposes. One might be designed to create employment, another to stimulate exports, a third to regenerate an underdeveloped area. Bear in mind too that many of the grants are industry-specific or area-specific. Furthermore, although some big sums are available (the European Grant Advisor Programme lists €15 million as the largest grant), the vast majority are worth between €5,000 and €100,000. Given this fact, unless you have a really brilliant concept it would be madness to let the 'grant tail' wag the 'business dog'. In other words, you should have a good business plan that would be viable whether or not you manage to get your hands on any grant funding.

Speaking of business plans, before you even start filling out applications you should get your paperwork in order. Whether you need a small grant to get a one-man-band off the ground or your company is looking for a large chunk of development capital, the rules are basically the same: detailed preparation and research pay dividends. Here's a check-list of some of the essential tasks:

- Research your market as effectively as possible. Who are your competitors and how will you compete against them? Learn as much as possible about the opportunities and threats facing your business.
- Know your own strengths and weaknesses. Make sure your own personal goals are in line with your business goals.
- Compile realistic financial projections. While tough

times are always likely in the early years, no-one is going to give a grant to a business that is never going to be able to pay its own way.

- Find out as much as you possibly can about potential grants in your area. Remember, moving a few miles down the road could open up a whole new avenue of free funds.
- Learn everything possible about the grants you are looking for. Watch out for closing dates (even if they are unofficial and not published).
- Prepare a business plan: you won't get very far without one.
- Review your plan for consistency. Is it coherent? Is it realistic? This is your guide to your business. It is what potential funders will use to assess your idea, and it will help you get what you want. Keep it updated. Change it as your goals change or as the market changes. Remember, a little planning will take you a long way.
- Be persistent. Even if they say no, don't give up. Reassess your strategy and try again. Often the grant-awarding body really wants to give you the money and is simply waiting for you to push the right button. Don't be afraid to ask what you need to do to get the money.
- You are not the first to try to get a grant and will certainly not be the last. Discover others who have been awarded grants and pick their brains to find out how they succeeded.

There are more than six hundred different grants available to Irish businesses, administered through a number of different grant-awarding bodies, including:

Arts Council
Grants for artists and art projects.
www.artscouncil.ie

An Bord Iascaigh Mhara (BIM)—Irish Sea Fisheries Board
Offers a small range of grants linked to the fishing industry.
www.bim.ie

County and City Enterprise Initiative
Feasibility grants, capital expenditure grants, employment grants and equity finance are all on offer.
www.enterpriseboards.ie; empower.ie

Department of Justice
Grants, believe it or not, for private child-care operators.
www.justice.ie

Department of Social and Family Affairs
Support to employers and employees designed to generate new jobs.
www.welfare.ie

Enterprise Ireland
Grants to manufacturing and internationally traded services companies employing more than ten people, as well as high-potential start-ups.
www.enterprise-ireland.com

FÁS—Training and Employment Authority
Offers a wide range of financial support to companies and individuals.
www.fas.ie

Leader
Leader is a European Community initiative for assisting rural communities in improving the quality of life and economic prosperity in their local area, and they hand out a great deal of money!
www.irishleadernetwork.org

Smurfit School of Hatchery
Grants of between €20,000 and €60,000 are available to graduates to help them start up a new venture.
ucdbusiness.ucd.ie

Údarás na Gaeltachta
Has the job of creating sustainable jobs and attracting investment to Irish-speaking districts and has generous financial incentives to entrepreneurs who are interested.
www.udaras.ie

If you want to know more about the grants offered by these and other organisations then visit the web sites listed below. All that free money is there and waiting for you—what a waste not to claim it!

European Union Grant Advisor
A fantastic site listing all six hundred available grants and offering free one-to-one help and support.
www.eugrantsadvisor.ie

Business Access to State Information and Services
Which is pretty self-explanatory! The Government's own list of available grants.
basis.ie

Industrial Development Authority (IDA)
Charged with attracting outside industry to Ireland.
idaireland.com

Department of Enterprise, Trade and Employment
Another very useful source of reference for the would-be grant applicant.
entemp.ie

Good luck with your plans. Don't put off till tomorrow what you can do today, and if the job is worth doing, it's worth doing well—these grants may just be the catalyst you are looking for.

Before making any financial decision you should always take professional advice.

(First published 10 September 2006)

25 EASY MONEY
MAKING A NET PROFIT

A s John Paul Getty, the oil billionaire, once observed, the only way to become seriously wealthy is to own your own business. Easy if you are entrepreneurial by nature, less easy if you are not. There is, however, one sort of business that can be set up without much capital and with little or no risk yet that has the potential to turn anyone into a multi-millionaire—a business, furthermore, that doesn't require experience or specialist skills and that can be started at home on a part-time basis. In fact all you need to get this business going is access to a computer with a broadband connection and a digital camera.

Ever since eBay was launched in 1994 the media have been full of stories about how ordinary individuals have become richer than their wildest dreams of avarice, thanks to the on-line auction site. Only this summer, for instance, the magazine *Entrepreneur* published a feature on ten young entrepreneurs (none over the age of thirty) who have built up vast international companies on eBay. A good example is Tiffany Tanaka, 24, who sells things through eBay on behalf of other people (www.wesellthings4U.com) and is now turning over $2.7 million a year. Another is David Wirtenberg, 28, who built up a $10 million jewellery business (www.outrageousdiamonds.com) from the sale of a single diamond ring on eBay in 2003.

What makes eBay such a fantastic money-making opportunity is its simplicity. Essentially it allows anyone, anywhere in the world, to buy or sell just about anything. The scale of the operation is mind-boggling. It sells a car every two minutes and a CD every seven seconds. Last time I checked there were more than 10 million items on offer and more than 168 million buyers. You could be selling to those 168 million buyers within minutes of finishing this article for, literally, a few euros. And selling for a very substantial profit too.

What could you be selling? Most new eBay entrepreneurs get started by auctioning unwanted items from their home. This can prove to be remarkably lucrative (I have a friend in west Cork who has made more than €3,000 since Christmas selling off unwanted clothes, books, children's toys and china) and also provides an opportunity to understand how eBay works. After you have the hang of it the secret is to find a product area that interests you. Different ideas include:

- dealing in something you know a lot about. Many people choose products related to their hobbies— everything from fishing rods to model trains
- selling something you can obtain elsewhere (possibly on the internet) for less
- selling for other individuals. Many of the most successful eBay sellers are simply selling other people's unwanted items on commission
- selling for other businesses. For instance, you could sell unwanted stock for local retailers.

As you become familiar with eBay you will start to see potential everywhere. Favourite categories include clothes and shoes, musical instruments, electronics and collectables—but the choice of products is endless. The most expensive item sold on the site to date was a Gulfstream aircraft for €3.8 million. Recently Ronan Keating's leather trousers went for €7,400—it didn't include Ronan.

Getting started, by the way, couldn't be easier. Last year eBay, which now has separate sites in thirty-three countries, was launched in Ireland, so all you need do is log on to www.eBay.ie and complete the on-line registration, which will ask you for a user name, password, e-mail address and credit card or debit card for verification purposes. This process won't cost you anything.

The next stage is to create a seller's account on line, for which you have to provide credit card or debit card details and bank account information for verification purposes. You then follow the listing instructions, giving product details, the duration of your listing—from one to ten days—and the starting and reserve price, if you want to set one. You have to pay a listing fee, which depends on the item's value and is a maximum of €3. If the item is sold you pay eBay a final value fee, which will be about 5.25% of the closing price.

Once you've joined you can sell anything with a few clicks of the mouse. To list your item you log in to the web site with your user identification, choose a category for your item, type in a description and details of how you propose to send the item to the buyer, and a price, and you're ready to start your auction.

You really need to include a digital photograph of the item, and the better your sales copy the greater the price you are likely to get. Once an item is listed, all you have to do is sit back and wait for the buyers to start bidding.

Most auctions last seven days, and the bidding can be

fierce—with much of it taking place in the last few minutes of the sale. If you want to optimise your chances of success you should always

- be honest about what you are selling
- write eye-catching advertisements and copy
- set a realistic starting price, or offer an item without any reserve price at all
- keep your buyer well informed
- don't despatch the goods until you have received payment.

Speaking of payment, eBay make it easy to collect money by means of a credit card, thanks to its own on-line payment system, which is called Paypal. In fact one of the best things about eBay is that it provides its sellers with plenty of support and advice. There is an eBay 'university', for instance, that holds both real and virtual courses; also an eBay 'community', where you can pick up information and tips from eBay 'power sellers'.

Its most useful resource is probably something called Seller Central, which is to be found at pages.ebay.com/ sellercentral. If you have a question about selling, the chances are that it will be answered here. This portal is divided into a handful of main categories, including getting started, best practices, advance selling and news and updates. Another useful sales advice section on the eBay site is to be found at pages.ebay.com/startselling.

Before making any financial decision you should always take professional advice.

(First published 17 September 2006)

26 | KISS KISS
HOME IMPROVEMENTS

How can you increase the value of your home or investment property regardless of what is happening to the market as a whole? The answer could well be to try a little kissing. The kiss principle—Keep it simple, stupid—reminds us that more often than not the most obvious ways to turn a profit are also the most lucrative. In this instance, what we are talking about is increasing the value of your property by making home improvements. Something as simple as upgrading your heating system or adding an extra bathroom could see you tens of thousands of euros richer.

Before we look at which improvements are (and aren't) worth making, let's just consider why now may be a good time to take action. It is not unreasonable to believe that we are entering a period of slower growth in house prices. True, there has been no sign of a slackening off yet, but sooner or later the effect of rising interest rates will have some impact. After all, a €250,000 mortgage costs €134 a month more now than it did at the end of last year, and could well cost as much again by the end of this year.

When growth does start to slow down, buyers will have more choice and—naturally—will look for homes with the features they really want. By adding those features now you can ensure that your property is more saleable—and more valuable—later. What's more, even if prices don't slow down as anticipated and the market continues to achieve the same levels of growth, you will still be better off. The right improvements will always add value.

There are two golden rules that you should remember when planning improvements. The first is not to spend more than you have to. Never improve a house to the point where its desired sale price would be more than, say, 20% higher than the most expensive of the other houses in the immediate neighbourhood. This is because the value of your home will always be affected (except in rural areas) by the value of the surrounding properties. The second is to ensure that any work carried out is of a professional standard. This is not the time to try out your DIY skills for the first time. Also, don't forget to keep all receipts and paperwork to show agents and prospective buyers.

One further point worth noting. The market is moving, increasingly, to the European and American way of valuing a house—that is to say, according to its usable area rather than the number of bedrooms. More square metres (or feet) means more money, so extra space should always reap you extra returns.

So, what's worth doing and what's not?

Heating. Installing central heating should add substantially to the value of your home. Gas, where available, is probably best—especially as oil prices are so high. If you are renovating or starting from scratch, underfloor heating is definitely worth the extra cost, as it means lower bills for your purchaser and no unsightly radiators.

Extra bedroom. The more the merrier is certainly the case when it comes to extra bedrooms—provided they are of a reasonable size. If you are going to the bother you might also consider adding a bathroom *en suite*. Buyers now demand more bathrooms.

Loft conversions and extensions. Extra space in a home almost always results in extra profit—provided the building work is of good quality, it is in keeping with the property and it doesn't push the value over the price parameters mentioned above.

Bathrooms. In principle, if you have a tired old bathroom it makes sense to upgrade it: underfloor heating, power showers etc. But potential buyers can be swayed either way by the look of a bathroom—so it can detract as well as add to the value. If in doubt when choosing a new bathroom, opt for white.

Windows. Replacing old windows, especially with double-glazed units, should more than pay for itself—provided the replacements are of good quality and in keeping with the house. If you are changing windows in a period property keep in the same style, and don't use modern upvc in any house that would originally have wooden windows. It's a price-killer.

Kitchens. Be as cautious about putting in a new kitchen as you would about putting in a new bathroom. If you are renovating a house, then obviously you must change the kitchen. But installing an expensive new kitchen just to sell your home is unlikely to repay the expense and bother.

A conservatory. As with anything that increases the total usable area in a house, a conservatory should definitely more than pay for itself. Shop around, as the market is notorious for huge price variations. Good ventilation, shade and heating are all important.

Parking. Somewhere to park the car (or cars)—especially in a busy urban area—is well worth arranging. So if you have an option of turning part of your front garden into a parking area, go for it, with the proviso that you should landscape it properly.

Luxury features. So what about roof terraces, saunas, Jacuzzis, gyms, wine cellars and similar features? Much depends on the location and size of your home. In general, however, spending money on such items is unlikely to produce a profit. In a quiet market one or two extra features may make your home more saleable—but anything that involves major expenditure is almost definitely not a good idea.

To be avoided. Interior design elements such as carpets, lighting, curtains, fitted furniture and so forth are all to be avoided at all costs, unless you are renovating a cheaply bought property from scratch. Don't even contemplate adding a swimming pool or tennis court: there's no money in them at all.

If you are planning to sell your home, remember that there are all sorts of ways to make it more attractive to buyers that won't necessarily result in much of a cash outlay. Sort out any minor odd jobs, like broken roof tiles; clean up around the outside of your home; remove clutter and give tired rooms a lick of paint.

The best way to pay for any home improvement is using savings, as it means you won't have the added expense of loan interest to bear—that's if you have savings in the first place. However, if you do need to borrow the most sensible way is to add the cost to your mortgage. By consolidating with your existing mortgage you will open up a whole new world of choice: forty-year terms, interest-only (even for the full forty years) current account mortgages, tracker rates, discounted rates. All in all, your house would get an uplift and so would your mortgage. A flexible mortgage may also attract, as it will allow you to make extra payments without penalty and thus save interest.

Finally, do not forget the actual land that your property is built on. Could you build another? Before making any financial decision you should always take professional advice.

(First published 15 October 2006)

27 | HAVE IT AWAY
EMERGING MARKETS AND HEDGE FUNDS

If you are interested in building up your wealth over the medium to long term, one of the best strategies you can employ is to put the vast majority of your capital into relatively safe investments (such as property and a pension) and a smaller amount into riskier but potentially more rewarding vehicles. If the higher-risk, higher-return investments do well they will substantially lift your overall worth. If they do less well they won't have any material effect on your standard of living.

The question is, of course, how to maximise the potential gain from these higher-risk investments without exposing yourself to undue loss. In recent years two possible means of doing this have attracted a great deal of publicity and cash. The first is investing in emerging markets; the second is investing in hedge funds. One is to be recommended, and the other isn't, as I am about to explain.

Did you know that the Russian stock market grew by a staggering 89.56% over the last year? Or that the Egyptian stock market grew by a no less impressive 57.98% a year over the last five years? Performance records in the emerging markets of eastern Europe, Asia, the Middle East and South America have been nothing short of spectacular. Furthermore, an impressive number of companies in these emerging markets are rapidly turning themselves from regional success stories into huge multinational conglomerates. As the *Investor's Chronicle* recently reported, 'if you are looking for decent, relatively cheap, relatively safe stocks you no longer have to limit your choice . . . the world is quite literally your oyster.'

Does it make sense, however, for a small, cautious private investor to put his or her hard-earned cash into this sector? For those who have already built up assets closer to home the answer could well be 'yes.' We live in a global economy, stock markets historically outperform all other forms of investment and one of the golden rules of making money is diversification. So, now could well be a very good time to start dipping your toe in rather more exotic foreign waters.

Why do emerging markets offer such good potential? I have already mentioned globalisation, and its effect should not be underestimated. The developed world depends for its own expansion on products and services purchased from the emerging economies. Growing political stability, developing equity markets and rapidly rising commodity prices all add to the attraction. It should also be noted that many companies are now listed not only on their local exchanges but also in London and New York.

What are the pitfalls? It is generally said that dips in the world's major stock markets spell long-term bad news for emerging market stocks. This may have been true in the past but is much less relevant nowadays. Many of the hotter markets, which suffered bad falls last May, have already bounced back. Anyway, it is a great mistake to lump all emerging markets together. Each one needs to be considered on its strengths and weaknesses, just as individual stocks do. There is a huge difference between, say, Thailand and Brazil, in the same way that there is a huge difference between, say, Delta and Ryanair.

How can you buy a little piece of the emerging market action? If you are willing to do the research you could invest directly. A good source of information is Boston Consulting's RDE 100 list. The initials 'RDE' stand for 'rapidly developing economies', and the list comprises a hundred firms from developing economies that are leading the pack when it comes to globalising their businesses. The list is to be found at www.bcg.com. Some are already global players, including such heavyweight names as CEMEX in Mexico (one of the world's largest cement-makers), Johnson Motors of Hong Kong (which has 40% of the global market for small electric motors), and Embraco of Brazil (which has 25% of the global market for compressors). Others already enjoy national or regional dominance and are now poised for global growth. They include Tata Motors of India, the Turkish consumer goods firm Vestel and Orascom Telecom in Egypt. Sixty of the firms on the list are, by the way, publicly quoted.

If you would prefer less direct involvement there are plenty of managed funds to pick from. The top performer for the last five years has been Credit Suisse European Frontiers, which is now showing a 292% gain.

A 292% gain over five years is just the sort of performance hedge fund managers have set out to achieve for their investors and many have achieved it—and better. Why, then, am I not promoting them as a good home for your cash? As the name suggests, a hedge fund is designed to strip out those risks that the fund's manager can't control—whether they relate to currencies, equities or geopolitical factors. Funds adopt different types of tactics to achieve their desired goal. These include macro funds, which seek to profit from changes in the global economy;

long and short equity funds, which invest in derivatives such as options and futures; and arbitrage funds, which aim to make a profit by buying one asset when it looks cheap and another when it looks expensive. All funds aim to make positive returns—net of fees—regardless of the direction of the markets.

When the concept was first dreamed up it made some sort of sense, and some funds justified the huge charges being made: management fees of 2% plus a 20% performance bonus above a certain watermark are not an uncommon. As funds have proliferated (there are now more than eight thousand in the world), though, it has become harder and harder for managers to achieve their objectives. My feeling that hedge funds have, largely speaking, had their day is confirmed by the way in which they are being sold on a mass scale to private investors. These investment vehicles were really designed for institutions, not individuals. When searching for something to spice up your portfolio of assets there are a lot of better places—not least the emerging economies—where you could look.

Before making any financial decision you should always take professional advice.

(First published 1 October 2006)

28 START SPREADING THE NEWS
SPREAD BETTING/DAY TRADING/COMMODITY TRADING

Have you ever been attracted by some of the more exciting financial opportunities often written about in the media? Spread betting, for instance? Day trading? Futures? Those promoting these strategies speak of the potential for massive gain. It is possible, they claim, to double, treble, quadruple your cash—or more—in the shortest possible time. The idea of making a vast profit in a matter of weeks, days, even hours is—of course—extremely tempting. So this week I thought I would explain how these much-publicised financial instruments work.

Spread betting has garnered a great deal of attention over the last few years. Its appeal lies in the fact that it allows you to bet cheaply on the rise or fall of an asset without actually owning it. Historically, if you wanted to trade in different markets—such as international shares, indices, property or commodities—you had to use a variety of different methods to do so. Not with spread betting. You can get exposure to a market instantly, with only a small deposit—typically about 10 to 20% of the value of your bet. In other words, a €1,000 bet could cost you as little as €100. What's more, there is no commission to be paid, no stamp duty on dealing and no tax to pay on winnings.

How does it work? A spread-betting firm will predict where an individual share or market will stand at a future date or period. They won't name a specific price but rather an upper and lower range. This range is referred to as the spread. You can then bet on the spread in one of two different ways. If you expect the share or market to be above the spread you can buy at the high end. If you expect the share or market to be below the spread you can opt for the low end.

This is best explained with an example. Supposing a spread-betting firm is quoting a spread of 6,100–6,110 for the FTSE 100 during January 2007. If you feel this is a bit pessimistic you might decide to bet €100 a point above 6,110. Any time before the end of January you can close your bet and take your gain or settle up your losses. Let's say you are right and the index climbs fifty points to 6,160, at which juncture you close the bet. You will collect €5,000 (50 points × €100). Let's say, on the other hand, you are wrong and the market falls fifty points below the top end of the spread to 6,060 (6,110 less 50). Your error of judgement is going to cost you €5,000! Basically, the more the market moves in your direction the more you stand to gain, and the more it moves against you the more you stand to lose. It is possible to limit your losses by paying for something called a 'guaranteed stop-loss', but the cost is usually so high as to make the chance of gain almost impossible.

Day trading first came into the news about six or seven years ago as a method by which small private investors could make money from the stock market. The name says it all. Day traders rapidly buy and sell stocks throughout the day in the hope that their stocks will continue climbing or falling in value for the seconds to minutes they own the stock, allowing them to lock in quick profits. It was the result of two phenomena. The first was greater market volatility, with the prices of some stocks—especially in the information technology sector—rising or falling by a substantial amount each day. The second was lower dealing charges, allowing investors to buy and sell for a relatively low cost. At the heart of the concept is the idea that you need to 'close your position' at the end of each trading day—taking your gains or losses then and there.

Putting your money into a futures or commodity contract also holds out the promise of substantial gain. As with spread betting, commodity trading involves predicting the price of a particular commodity—anything from gold to frozen orange juice, from silver to pork bellies—at a specific point in the future. And, as with spread betting, gearing plays a big factor in the activity. Its history, however, is rather more respectable.

These contracts were originally a way for manufacturers to reduce their risk. For instance, in the days when silver was more important to the photographic industry than it is in this digital age a company such as Kodak might contract to buy a set amount of the metal a year before it actually needed it at an agreed price. On making the contract it would traditionally pay a deposit—usually 10% of the total contract value. Before long it was realised that this was a way in which anyone—not just manufacturers—might make a great deal of money. How? Like this. Let's say you think silver is going to go up in price. You pay €10,000 to purchase a €100,000 contract. If you are right and silver goes up 10% you make €10,000—doubling your money.

On the other hand, if silver falls 10% you lose your €10,000. And if it falls 20% you would lose an additional €10,000.

You may have noticed that in describing these three different methods by which it is possible to make—or lose—a small fortune I have not once used the words 'investment' or 'investor'. Spread betting, day trading and futures are all out-and-out gambles. Putting your cash into any of them is no different from putting your cash on a horse—not to be recommended to anyone wishing to increase rather than decrease their wealth.

There is, however, one speculation that I might recommend to anyone who wants a chance of getting rich quick: prize bonds. You can invest as little as €25 and your capital is 100% secure. Every month you will be in the running for up to ten thousand prizes worth anything from €75 to €150,000; and since 2.4% of the prize fund size is paid out per annum, statistically you have a better chance of coming away with something regularly, and a much greater chance than investing in the lottery!

Before making any financial decision you should always take professional advice.

(First published 19 November 2006)

29 | **MINTING IT**
NUMISMATICS—COIN COLLECTING

The first coins invented were probably stamped ingots of electrum, a mixture of gold and silver, created by the Lydians, a people of Asia Minor, in about 650 BC. The most famous Lydian was King Croesus, who introduced pure gold coins and was the inspiration behind the expression 'as rich as Croesus.'

Will you become as rich as Croesus yourself if you invest in coins? With careful planning the answer could well be in the affirmative, because, according to the specialists Noble Investments, long-term coin collections spanning a period of fifty years or more have achieved compound annual returns of 8.7 to 10.5% a year—which certainly matches or betters just about every major stock market in the world. Furthermore, short-term performance has also been strong. A random portfolio of gold and silver coins selected from Spink's auction catalogue in 2000 would have shown a compound annual return of 12%.

As Mark Twain pointed out, there are three kinds of lies: lies, damned lies and statistics; but there is plenty of other evidence to suggest that coins would at present make an addition to any investment portfolio. 'Investment-quality coins are in the early stages of a long-awaited major upswing,' according to Barry Stuppler, publisher of the magazine *Coin Connoisseur*. 'Investors have responded to recent stock market declines and geo-political strife by retreating to safe-haven assets, including metals. Collectable coins should demand even higher premiums because they are in such short supply.' His optimism is shared by Peter Temple of the *Financial Times*, who recently wrote that 'the higher levels of inflation now becoming apparent in western economies are making collectables such as stamps and coins almost a no-brainer.'

Nor must it be forgotten that the coin market is both global and relatively liquid. A rare coin is easy to store and transport, and it can be sold quickly and inexpensively anywhere in the world, thanks to a plethora of collectors, dealers, auction houses and the internet—something that cannot be said of many alternative investments. Added to which there is the pleasure of collecting something of intrinsic interest. Numismatics offers a fascinating link with the past and offers an excuse to study everything from history to economics and from theology to metallurgy.

Coins are an art form too. It is generally considered that the masterpieces of the coin world were produced in the Greek colony of Sicily in the fifth and fourth centuries BC. Take a silver decadrachm struck in Syracuse around 400 BC. The work of Euainetos, its obverse features a fast quadriga driven by a female charioteer. The sense of speed is achieved by two of the horses slightly rearing and the hooves—all of which are above the ground—forming a jagged broken pattern. A coin such as this is, frankly, a thing of great beauty as well as of great value.

What sort of coins should you invest in to optimise your returns? There are two approaches you could take. The first is to diversify, buying the best examples you can afford in a wide range of different categories—everything from ancient Greek coinage to modern commemorative sets. The benefit of this strategy is that the value of your collection will not be vulnerable to the vagaries of fashion.

On the other hand, it is not necessarily as interesting, as specialising in one or more areas you may miss out on the spectacular growth that can be achieved with a little speculative foresight. For example, up until the late 1970s little attention was paid to the intriguing Islamic coinages of the Middle East. Arabs themselves were not attracted to their past coinage, and consequently the market for Islamic coins was confined to a small band of dedicated scholars and collectors. However, all this altered when Arabs developed a growing awareness of their cultural heritage and began to form collections of numismatic treasures.

Should you decide to build up a collection you could do so by choosing a theme (such as coins featuring a particular animal), a *type* (the technical term for a main design of coin, issued in a particular country, state or region), a denomination (such as gold sovereigns), a ruler (collecting an example of a coin from each reign of an emperor, king or queen), or commemoratives (coins that were struck to celebrate particular events).

Possibly you may be drawn by the idea of collecting Irish coins, and this certainly offers plenty of scope. The first Irish coinage was the so-called Hiberno-Norse coinage, which was first minted in Dublin in about 995 AD under the authority of Sithric III (also known as Sithric Silkbeard), the Norse king of Dublin. So, if you try and start at the beginning you have more than a thousand years of history to collect from.

I have already mentioned that you should always buy the best example you can afford. The commercial value of any coin depends on four factors:

(1) its exact design, legend, mintmark or date
(2) its exact state of preservation
(3) the demand for it in the market at any given time
(4) the availability of similar coins in the market at that time.

Interestingly, the appearance on the market of newly discovered examples of a coin or of a long-held private collection seems to have the effect of pushing prices up. Even though the supply of available coins has been increased at a stroke, demand rises proportionately more. This situation has become more noticeable in recent years, emphasising the fact that quality coins are becoming more difficult to find. The market has never experienced a state of saturation on the disposal of a quality collection—which is good news for investors.

There are so many possible sources of reference for anyone interested in investing in coins that it is hard to know where to start. For Irish coins I would certainly recommend visiting www.irishcoinage.com, which includes a complete illustrated history. If you want to know more about the market in general try www.noble investmentsplc.co.uk—the only numismatic trading and investment company listed on the stock market in Britain. The biggest and longest-established coin dealer in the world is probably Spink and Son, which, as you would expect, has a superb web site (www.spinkandson.com). It also publishes a fantastic range of reference books on the subject.

One final tip. Prices tend to be highest in the country of origin, which means if you search overseas you may find better deals—especially where the euro is stronger than the local currency. Do, however, be cautious about buying from individuals or over the internet. Better to pay slightly more and know you are investing in the genuine article.

(First published 8 October 2006)

30 | FLOAT YOUR BOAT

BUSINESS OPPORTUNITIES IN A FOREIGN CLIME

A 35-acre award-winning vineyard in Romania, complete with mini-castle and winery for under €460,000. A productive 10-acre organic olive grove with villa on an unspoilt Greek island for €275,000. A yacht charter business based in the Mediterranean and generating a gross annual profit of €150,000 for €500,000. A successful seaside restaurant with living accommodation and sunny terrace in Majorca for €650,000. A small, popular bar in Marbella with studio apartment for €95,000. A 700-acre equestrian centre—including private airstrip and plane—in New Zealand for €1.2 million. A motel with a stunning 1930s swimming pool and development potential in Miami for €1.9 million.

Tempted by any of the above? One of the many benefits of our booming economy and buoyant property market is that life-style businesses overseas now represent incredible value for money. For the price of a relatively modest suburban home in Dublin you can buy a fantastic—and lucrative—life-style business in any number of desirable locations elsewhere in the world. With a slightly larger sum you can afford something truly stupendous and potentially even more profitable.

There's so much choice too. Move abroad—perhaps to a warmer, drier climate—and enjoy running the business yourself. Or stay here in Ireland and employ someone else to manage it for you. Opt for a venture that allows you to work from home (bearing in mind that that 'home' could well be a dream property) or keep the two separate.

Identifying life-style business opportunities in foreign climes is anything but difficult. Thanks to the worldwide web and Google it took me less than fifteen minutes to search out the opportunities above. Nor need funding be an issue. Finding the money to invest in overseas property is both easy and relatively inexpensive. You could use equity built up in an existing property, capital held elsewhere or possibly borrow on the strength of the business itself. All you need do is talk to your financial adviser. Nor, in these days of budget air travel and low-cost communications, need moving abroad mean losing touch with family and friends.

So, what are the main considerations for anyone attracted by the idea of a business place in the sun? For some, the first question will be what sort of business to buy, for others it will be the location. Either way, you need to weigh up

- your interests and skills. If this is going to be a proper life-style business then you need to pick something you will enjoy doing
- how you feel about the local culture. The thrill of owning, say, an Austrian ski-resort hotel might be somewhat dulled if you aren't that keen on life in Austria
- whether the business will produce sufficient returns for your needs. This is particularly relevant if you want to

employ other people to run it
* the potential for capital gain. It clearly makes sense to purchase something that—regardless of annual profits—is likely to increase in value.

One area to be especially mindful of is overcapitalising certain types of business. Take, for instance, someone who buys a large period property in, say, France and over several years turns it into a successful restaurant with holiday accommodation. When it comes to selling, the combined value of the property and the business may be so great as to make it difficult to find a sufficiently well-off buyer interested in running this type of venture.

Not that it doesn't make much more sense to opt for a business incorporating a freehold property. Yes, it might be fun to run a leasehold night-club in Ibiza; but you've less to sell should you ever get bored with being surrounded by an endless stream of young, beautiful people intent on having a good time.

Other important factors to weigh up when making an overseas business investment include:
* the tax climate. Watch out for higher stamp duty, income tax and capital gains tax. Also beware of death duties. Always take professional tax advice before you commit yourself to anything.
* the legal climate. Not only can ownership be less clear-cut in other jurisdictions (even within the EU) but also many countries have different inheritance rules. Again, take legal advice before you commit yourself to anything.
* the regulatory climate. Ever tried to get a business licence in Spain? Or a work permit in Malta? Or even something as simple as planning permission in France? Make sure you will be able to do what you want with

your business (and that you know what you are letting yourself in for).

- the work climate. Your grand plans for a business may come to nothing if you can't find the employees and contractors you need to make your dream come true.
- the language. Hardly a problem if you opt for an English-speaking country—but elsewhere? There are some places—the Netherlands and most Spanish coastal resorts, to name two—where you can get away without a word of the local language. Otherwise you should either speak—or plan to learn to speak—the language.
- employment and residence issues. As an Irish citizen you can move anywhere you want within the EU. Many other countries, including the United States, will welcome you with open arms if you are making an appropriate investment.

Once you have found a business you are interested in then it is important to get an independent, reliable valuation. What can seem a bargain when compared with Irish prices may not be so much of a bargain to local people. Pay special attention to the history of the business; its current performance (sales, turnover and profit); its financial situation (cash flow, debts, expenses and assets); and why the business is being sold. Once you have agreed a price don't hesitate to get 'due diligence'—the process of checking that everything you have been told is true.

Is it sensible to invest your cash in a life-style business overseas? Bear in mind that you are taking a double risk: firstly, that the business itself is sound and that you will be successful running it; secondly, that the country where you are buying it won't experience a downturn. This said, we may well be at the top of our economic cycle, whereas many suitable locations may be near the bottom of theirs. This type of diversification could, therefore, make excellent sense.

Before making any financial decision you should always take professional advice.

(First published 22 October 2006)

31 | RED LIGHT, GREEN CASH
INVESTING IN THE ENVIRONMENT

Here's a prediction. In the next few years, as climate change moves up the political agenda, you will be offered endless opportunities to invest in something called 'carbon-emission credits'. You will be able to invest directly, in the same way that you might buy a commodity such as gold or oil, and indirectly, through unit trusts, tracker funds and other vehicles. Every financial institution in the developed world will jump onto the bandwagon, carbon emission credits will become the next 'big thing' and the price will move rapidly upwards.

This, as you can imagine, will bring a smile to the faces of those who had the foresight to get in early when prices were rock-bottom low. Actually, it is difficult to imagine that prices will be any lower than they are right now, because the carbon-emission credit market is still so new that barely anyone knows of its existence, making it an ideal investment for anyone who can afford to risk a modest amount of cash on something that could well provide astronomical returns.

One of the reasons why carbon-emission credits remain

a relatively unknown investment opportunity is that very few people have taken the trouble to understand what they are or how they work. Their history dates from the Kyoto summit in 1991, at which many of the world's countries, including all the countries of the EU, agreed to cut the amount of greenhouse gases—carbon dioxide, methane, nitrous oxide and fluorocarbons—that are being pumped into the atmosphere. These gases are significant catalysts of global warming, which is responsible for triggering severe changes in weather conditions.

Under European regulations, all member-states have a cap on the amount of carbon they may now produce. This allowance is distributed among all the major carbon-producers, such as energy companies, major manufacturers and so forth. If a business produces more carbon than permitted it must purchase extra credits from 'cleaner' companies that have not used up their quota. In other words, the EU has created a trading scheme by which companies can buy and sell carbon-emission credits.

What is happening in Europe is happening in other parts of the world too. Furthermore, in developing economies companies that use environmentally responsible production methods will be given 'certified emission reduction' (CER) credits, which may be sold to businesses in developed countries that have been unable to reach their emission targets.

The market in carbon-emission credits is still in its infancy and might be regarded as particularly high-risk were it not for a number of crucial factors. To begin with, the level of carbon credits allocated to each country will be reduced every year as the EU attempts to meet its greenhouse gas targets. This will mean that the demand for credits will go up. Secondly, the EU—though shamefully slow in tackling climate change—has been leading the world in carbon trading. As other countries, such as the United States, which has still not signed up to the Kyoto protocol, start to seek ways to offset their carbon emissions, the market is likely to further expand.

What of prices? At present a CER costs between €7 and €8, and it is anticipated that the price will rise to between €12 and €20 after 2008, when EU emission rules become somewhat stricter. Another way to look at the market, however, is to consider the volume of credits being traded. The amount of traded EU units—one unit representing the right to emit one tonne of carbon—in May this year was 53 million, compared with only 1 million the previous year. One analyst expected that between 2008 and 2012, 10 billion units would be traded each year, compared with only 260 million in 2005.

There are a number of different methods by which a private investor can gain entry to this market. These include:

- investing in a niche fund. To give you three examples: a fund called Icecap, which acts as a hedging tool for utilities firms worried about the price of carbon-emission credits rising too quickly; the Renewable Energies Fund operated by Triodos, the ethical bank; or one of the funds run by Climate Change Capital (www.climatechangecapital.com).

- buying into a carbon reduction project. This will provide you with a share of the emission-reduction certificates awarded to the project—which you can then hold or sell on. To find suitable projects it is best to deal with a broker. Two possible brokers to approach are Evolution Markets (www.evomarkets.com) and TFS (www.tfsbrokers.com).

- starting your own carbon-reduction scheme and then selling on the credits this generates. For instance, you might finance the replanting of an area of logged rainforest. One organisation to talk to about this is the World Land Trust (www.worldlandtrust.org); however, you will need a substantial amount of capital to make this worth while.

Another option might be to invest in companies or funds set to benefit from carbon-emission credits or from the switch to alternative, clean sources of energy. Though I don't advise it, you may also be interested to know that it is possible to place a spread bet on the price of carbon through IG Index.

What are the risks involved in buying and selling carbon credits? Obviously, prices can fall as well as rise. Also, this is a nascent market and the EU may eventually decide to do away with the trading scheme. Nevertheless, I still predict that carbon-emission credits will be one of the hottest investment opportunities of the next decade. If you would like to learn more then I can recommend two excellent web sites. The first is operated by the World Bank (www.carbonfinance.org); the second is run by the RSA (www.rsa.org).

Before making any financial decision you should always take professional advice.

(First published 12 November 2006)

32 | MONEY GROWS ON TREES
FORESTRY INVESTMENT

Here's a way of making money that is as easy as falling off a log. Ireland is the least afforested country in the EU. Only 10% of our land mass is covered in trees, compared with an EU average of 38%. This is such bad news from both an environmental and economic viewpoint that the government behaves with uncharacteristic generosity to anyone willing to invest in forestry. In fact if you decide to put your cash into timber your only expense should be the cost of buying suitable land. This is because there are 100% grants for planting, maintaining and improving forests as well as, where relevant, generous compensation for any loss of farm income. What's more, any profit generated from forestry is 100% tax-free.

But will your forestry investment generate a profit? Let me reassure you that it isn't just the grants and tax breaks that have turned forestry into an attractive money-making opportunity. The returns from timber are remarkably high. If you look at American performance figures since 1910, for instance, timber has done better than the Standard and Poor Index. In Ireland, average annual growth for the sector runs—over the medium to long term—at 5 to 7%, net of inflation, with a hectare of timber at present yielding as much as €15,000. There is also the very real possibility in the near future of additional gains in the form of carbon credits: basically, as a forest owner you could get paid for improving the environment and helping to slow down climate change.

The benefits of investing in forestry can, therefore, be summarised as follows:

* Excellent prospect of above-average returns.
* The reassurance of knowing your money is invested in a physical asset.
* Low risk. The market for timber has been steadily growing and there is every reason to believe that the rising demand will continue.
* Generous government grants keep the costs down to a minimum.
* The potential of extra windfalls from carbon credits.
* It is an ethical investment.
* It would make a sound addition to a pension fund.
* Any income generated is tax-free.

With regard to the tax benefits it is worth noting that under existing legislation 'distributions to the extent that they represent profits from the occupation of woodland managed on a commercial basis are exempt from income and corporation tax.' However, in the Finance Act (2006), 'where an investor avails of reliefs or exemptions from tax in any year, which in aggregate exceed €250,000, a restriction of reliefs shall apply.' In other words, there is a cap on the amount of tax-free profits you can take—but this will only affect you if your tax-exempt income is over a quarter of a million euros in any one year.

What of the risks? Forestry is not a liquid asset, and if

you wish to dispose of an investment—whether held directly or indirectly—you may not be able to do it immediately. Furthermore, to optimise your gains you should probably think of waiting a decade or longer before realising your profits. On the other hand, you will be reassured to know that forestry does not seem to be much affected by economic downturns. Trees were the only asset class to go up in value during three of the four market collapses of the twentieth century.

Another advantage of forestry is that there is a range of direct and indirect investment options. The direct route requires more capital, because you will need to fund the purchase of a reasonable area of land. You will also require sufficient cash to meet planting and maintenance costs until grant money comes through. You won't, however, have to become intimately involved with your investment—unless you wish to. There are a number of specialist forest management companies (see below) that will be only too pleased to oversee everything from helping you to choose appropriate land to applying for grants, and from planting to continuing management.

One decision you will need to take is whether to go for 'bare' land or semi-mature forest. The cost of bare land has been rising because of competing land uses and speculative investment. Be aware too that there are useful stamp duty exemptions on land that has already been planted.

If you don't have sufficient capital or the inclination to purchase your own wood or forest, the other option is to buy into a forestry investment fund. The most successful of these is run by Irish Forestry, which trades as IFS Asset Managers Ltd. IFS has so far attracted more than 14,400 individuals to its various investment funds—all of which sell out relatively quickly. Its last fund, for instance, was designed to run for twelve years and offered a projected return of 8.5% compound per annum tax-free. The minimum investment was just €750 per unit. Its next fund is due to be launched any day now. If you want details, drop me an e-mail message.

If you are interested in the idea of investing in forestry there is plenty of information available—much of it from the government and non-profit organisations. I would definitely recommend contacting the Department of Agriculture and Food, which has a special Forestry Service, or visiting its web site at www.agriculture.gov.ie. Another useful resource is Coillte (www.coillte.ie), a private company that took over running all state forests in 1989 and that is happy to advise private investors. Coillte also offers a complete management service to farmers and landowners. You should also contact the Irish Timber Growers' Association (www.itga.ie), which provides valuable support services to its members.

Before making any financial decision you should always take professional advice.

(First published 26 November 2006)

33 | RIGHT ON TRACK
TRACKER FUNDS

What is the greatest investment vehicle invented in the last hundred years, and how can you make serious money from it? A couple of weeks ago it was the thirtieth birthday of what I consider to be one of the least-known but most innovative financial products ever devised: the index fund.

On the face of it there is nothing especially thrilling about index funds, which are also known as tracker funds. Their purpose is to mimic—or track—the performance of one of the indices that are used to indicate market movement. For example, a fund designed to mimic the ISEQ Equity Index (the index that measures the Irish Stock Exchange performance) would hope to match every rise (and fall) of the market. Index funds achieve their results by replicating the behaviour of the chosen index throughout the day—buying and selling each share or type of share in proportion to the market. In other words, if, say, AIB's stock made up 1% of the market, 1% of the index fund would consist of AIB shares.

So far, so prosaic. The huge advantage of index funds, however, from a private investor's viewpoint is that they offer a way of matching what the market is doing, without having to invest in every single relevant stock. This in turn means plenty of diversification, less risk, and lower costs.

There was no wild celebration when the index fund hit the big three-o, but it served as a good reminder that if you want to build up some serious wealth—safely and securely—you must make sure that you are sufficiently exposed to the stock market. Why? Because, compared with any other investment you care to name—from property to gold and from art to oil—over the medium to long term nothing has ever matched the profit potential of publicly quoted stocks and shares. The Irish market, for instance, which is by no means the highest-performing market in the world, has produced gains of 62% over the last five years, 222% over the last ten years and 856% over the last twenty years! Compare with the S&P 500: 477% growth over the last twenty years, while the FTSE 100 grew 286% over the same period.

How much of your net worth should be invested in the stock market depends on your personal circumstances. Ideally, by the time you retire it would probably be wise to have no more than a third of your capital tied up in your main home, with the rest in other investments.

You may actually have more exposure to the market already than you realise. If you have a pension fund the chances are that a large percentage of it will be invested in the market, and the same is true of many life insurance policies. This will be in addition, of course, to any managed funds you may have bought into and any directly held shares. Whatever your exposure, it is pretty likely that putting money into one or more index funds will still make sound sense.

One thing is certain: you won't be alone. A leading expert recently estimated that about 25% of the world's entire stock of professionally managed money is now held in index funds of one kind or another. The first index fund was launched by Jack Bogle, a professional investor. In 1976 he found himself without a job and decided to go into business for himself, launching an investment firm called Vanguard. His first fund was the Vanguard s&p 500, and its aim was to replicate the performance of the Standard and Poor top 500 shares. For many years his concept was ridiculed by competitors and the media. Indeed it wasn't until the early 1980s that other money managers finally began to imitate him. Now there are, literally, thousands of funds in the same sector—though it has to be said that the Vanguard s&p 500 remains one of the most impressive. In the last thirty years it has produced a compound annual return of 12% each year.

There are two types of index fund: exchange-traded funds (ETFS) and index mutual funds. ETFS are, basically, funds that are themselves traded on a stock exchange. If you want to invest in such a fund you simply buy shares in it. Index mutual funds, on the other hand, can only be invested in through a professional adviser or direct with the managers. In both categories there are, literally, thousands of funds around the world to choose from.

The first thing to decide is what sort of index you want your investment to reflect. The options open to you include *broad market indices* (such as the Wiltshire 5000 in the United States, which covers the entire public equity market), *large cap* (cap for 'capitalisation' or the worth of a company), *stock indices, mid cap stock indices,* and *small cap stock indices*—each of which focuses on public companies with similar levels of market capitalisation. You could also consider *growth and value indices* (based on expected long-term earnings growth), *international indices,* and *bond indices.*

It is worth noting that index funds usually do not buy

every underlying security in a given index but may instead buy a selection of securities whose performance closely tracks that of the index as a whole. Because they do not engage in costly investment research—and because they tend to trade less often than actively managed funds—index funds usually have lower expenses than actively managed funds. This is why some index funds are able to offer lower fees.

There are many index funds in Ireland, obtainable primarily through insurance companies—notably Irish Life PLC, which introduced the first ten years ago—so it is well worth studying their performance before opting for any particular fund. Alternatively, you should discuss your needs with your professional adviser.

Before making any financial decision you should always take professional advice.

(First published 17 December 2006)

34 | GIVE ME A SIGN
HISTORIC DOCUMENTS
AND AUTOGRAPHS

W hy shouldn't making money be fun as well as lucrative? In 1997 you would have paid €180 for a signed photograph of Paul McCartney. In 2005 the same photograph would have cost you €1,800—an increase of 900% in eight years. Shares, property, managed funds, commodities—they all have their place in a well-balanced portfolio and they all offer the active investor something to get his or her teeth into.

No matter how profitable or interesting each of these areas may prove, however, none of them could really be described as entertaining. Which is why I have recently become a convert to philography—the process of collecting autographs and signed historical documents. Here is a money-making activity—the sheer potential for gain may surprise you—that is both enjoyable and intellectually stimulating, a money-making activity, furthermore, that can involve putting your cash into something as serious as an original Proclamation of the Irish Republic from 1916 or as frivolous as one of Marilyn Monroe's black nylon stockings.

There is nothing new about the idea of collecting

autographs: its history can be traced back to the sixteenth century and before. What is new, though, is the way in which the market has expanded and stabilised, as evidenced by the number of regular auctions held in large cities throughout the world. This year in Dublin, for instance, there have been several major sales, the most important being staged by Adams last April. Record prices were achieved for a range of documents and historical treasures relating to the turbulent birth of modern Ireland. These included Michael Collins's typewriter and an essay he wrote on 'Ancient and modern warfare' at the age of 14, collections of Patrick Pearse's letters and poetry, and the first handwritten draft of 'The Soldier's Song', which made €760,000. Not that you have to be incredibly wealthy to invest. At other Dublin sales this year you could have picked up a handwritten letter by Daniel O'Connell to his son for €800, a letter by Thomas Moore to his publisher for €380, or a signed photograph of the band Them—fronted by Van Morrison in the 1960s—for under €100.

The reason for all this auction-house activity is the sheer number of collectors. The days when the market was supported by a dwindling band of dedicated enthusiasts are long gone. It is estimated that there may be as many as 48 million collectors in the world, and growth has been fuelled by, among other things, strong Russian and Chinese demand for items connected with iconic western figures and the shift in demographics being experienced in many developed countries. The effect of affluent 'baby boomers' coming into retirement and looking for an interesting hobby, in particular, should not be underestimated. Also, autographs and historical documents have scarcity value as well as being portable and easy to store—making them an ideal way to hold wealth for those in unstable or highly taxed jurisdictions.

Alternative investments, such as philography, are only appropriate, of course, for those who have other assets, such as a home and pension. It must be remembered too that past performance is no guide to future performance. This said, the Fraser's 100 Index—which tracks the price of a hundred typical autographs from year to year—has shown stupendous gains since it was started in 1997. Over the last eight years the total value of the hundred examples has risen from €117,000 to €356,000. This represents a return of 204%, or 14.9% a year. The index is run by Fraser's Autographs (www.frasersautographs.co.uk), which is part of the Stanley Gibbons Group. Stanley Gibbons has been trading in collectables for more than 150 years, so they certainly know how to take the long-term view. The group recently launched an autograph investment division, offering a guaranteed annual return of 6% over ten years.

The minimum investment is €7,500 (£5,000). Its experts will build a portfolio for you and store and insure it without charge. At the end of the term you can opt to (a) take the guaranteed return, (b) sell your portfolio for 75% of the catalogue price, (c) sell it commission-free at auction or (d) keep it—as you prefer. Interestingly, one of their clients is Michael Forbes, publisher of the magazine *Forbes*, who says that 'none of my other investments give me the joy that autographs do, because they make me feel that I am holding a piece of history in my hand.'

Indeed it is this sense that one is preserving history that seems to motivate many collectors. Signed letters, documents, manuscripts, books and photographs all bring a moment to life, often with incredible power. Whether you collect letters from political figures, musical scores by great composers or pictures of famous actors with illuminating inscriptions, autographs offer valuable insights into the thoughts and aspirations of those who shaped history.

If you plan to invest in this sector the first thing to decide is what sort of collection is going to interest you. Avoid fads or anything that is too readily available and learn as much as you can about what makes an autograph authentic and important. While diversification is important, remember that the best examples will always command the best prices. Therefore, concentrate on a small number of good autographs rather than a larger collection of mediocre examples.

Don't forget either that autographs fade if exposed to light, so although it is fun to have signed, framed photographs of well-known personalities or historic documents all over your house, it probably isn't a good idea. Finally, take advantage of the many knowledgeable dealers. This is an area where it pays to listen to specialist advice.

Before making any financial decision you should always take professional advice.

(First published 10 December 2006)

35 | VROOM FOR INVESTMENT
CLASSIC MOTOR BIKES

I f any of the following—BSA, BMW, Ducati, Harley-Davidson, Honda, Norton, Triumph or Yamaha—cause your pulse to quicken, then here is some news that will gladden your heart: for the first time ever the classic motorcycle market has been experiencing strong and steady growth. As a result, buying the bike you always coveted could prove to be a very solid investment. Of course, not all classic motorbikes are going to accelerate in price at the same speed—but choose cannily and you could be sitting on some very rapid profits.

Until a few years ago the price of classic motorcycles roughly kept pace with inflation. Then, unexpectedly, interest began to grow from three quite separate quarters. Firstly, middle-aged riders who hadn't been able to afford a motorbike in their youth started to buy machines they had always dreamt of owning. Secondly, younger riders who had only experienced modern machines came to appreciate the pleasures of driving something older and more graceful. Thirdly, potential classic car buyers started to realise the benefits of two wheels over four. The result? The lower and medium ends of the market have been showing price increases of between 10 and 20% a year, while the top end of the market has been growing at about 20 to 30% a year.

It is easy to understand the attraction of owning a classic motorcycle. To begin with, the initial investment is so much lower. Prices start at a few hundred euros, and a budget of between €3,000 and €15,000 will buy you something special—even if the most expensive models are now in the six-figure bracket. Classic bikes are considerably easier to maintain than classic cars: the engineering is simpler and there is so much less to go wrong. What's more, thanks to an extensive range of clubs, dealers and parts manufacturers, there are few mechanical problems that can't be solved quickly and relatively inexpensively.

It must also be said that classic bikes tend not to seize up in the same way as classic cars if you don't drive them regularly. And, of course, they don't require much storage space. No wonder, perhaps, that many well-known personalities, including Gay Byrne, Larry Mullen, Nicky Koumarianos and Justin McCarthy, have long been classic motorcycle enthusiasts.

The history of the motorcycle can be traced back to the beginnings of the twentieth century. In its early years the market was very much dominated by the British. Between 1900 and the 1950s there were more than a hundred different British marques. In the mid-1970s, however, their motorcycle industry effectually came to an end and it was the Germans, Americans, Italians and—especially—Japanese who enjoyed world dominance. This means that potential investors are faced with a huge range of choice. If the primary object is making money, where should one look?

There is much to be said for buying British for geographical reasons alone: lower transport costs and greater access to mechanical support and parts when compared with, say, Japan or the United States. It is possible to buy a famous marque, such as a BSA Bantam, in running order for as little as €700; and the same sort of money will buy you something much more interesting for restoration. Spend between €3,000 and €8,000, say, and you will be able to get your hands on a good twin-cylinder Triumph or Norton that will be ready for the road.

Although it is likely that bikes in this price range will show modest growth, if you are keen to see more spectacular gains you won't want to confine yourself to a British marque. What you'll be looking for is rarity, a significant racing history and immaculate provenance. A good example would be the Honda RC164 racer ridden by the world champion Jim Redman during the 1964 season, the 1976 Suzuki RG500 raced by the late Barry Sheene, or a German Munch-URS grand prix racer built by the company for the 1970 racing season. Bikes such as these command prices of between €150,000 and €700,000 and invariably exceed their estimates when sold at auction.

Whatever your budget, there are some golden rules you should always follow when considering a purchase:

- Get expert advice. It is important that what you buy is genuine and original. The engine and frame numbers should match and all the parts should be correct. Be wary of fakes.
- Better to purchase something original with a provenance (especially long single ownership) and that is mechanically sound than a bike that has been restored but owned by more than one person.
- If the bike was expensive when it was sold new, it is more likely to increase in value in the future.
- Innovative, well-engineered bikes will also show more growth potential.

Auctions are one of the best places to find suitable purchases, because provenance is more or less guaranteed. Bonham's (www.bonhams.com) has established itself as the largest international auction house specialising in classic motorcycles, with sales held regularly in Britain and the United States. The best-known American auction house is Mid-America Auctions (www.midamericaauctions.com) in Las Vegas. Ron Christensen, the company's spokesman, recently reported that they expect to sell more than five hundred bikes in a single weekend this coming January; sales have doubled over the last five or six years. Established dealers also have much to be said in their favour, as they will be keen to protect their reputations and can also advise on restoration, storage and maintenance.

If you are keen to learn more then there are a number of excellent magazines worth subscribing to, including *Classic Bike* and *Classic Bike Guide* (www.classicbikeguide.co.uk) and *Classic Motorcycle* (www.classicmagazines.co.uk). A list of events can be found on the Classic Shows web site (www.classicmagazines.co.uk), and I would also recommend investing in a copy of the *New Illustrated Encyclopaedia of Motorcycles* by Erwin Tragatsch and Kevin Ash (Greenwich Editions). Do bear in mind that a classic motorcycle is an alternative investment and you should only buy if you have already invested in more traditional areas, such as property or the stock market.

Before making any financial decision you should always take professional advice.

(First published 21 January 2007)

36 SNOW BUSINESS
SKI RESORT PROPERTY

There is no business like snow business when it comes to investing in ski resort property. Buy in the right location and you could enjoy capital appreciation of up to 33% a year, rental yields of around 5% a year and the opportunity to enjoy inexpensive holidays on the slopes thrown in. Buy in the wrong location, however, as some investors have found to their cost, and you'll see your chances of profit melting away. Which is a shame, because when it comes to making money, ski properties offer the potential for some very cool gains.

What should a canny investor be looking for? The main consideration is the quality and quantity of the snow. Because of the effects of climate change, it is important to buy at sufficiently high altitude to ensure a long, reliable season. For this reason such locations as Cyprus and Turkey are probably not a good idea. Anyway, ski enthusiasts want more than just snow: they want a good range of challenging runs as well as first-class facilities. With regard to the latter, if there aren't well-maintained, convenient lifts, forget it. You should probably also rule out anywhere that is difficult to get to; proximity to an airport definitely adds value.

Having said this, one of the resorts I am going to suggest

in a moment is Niseko in Japan. Why? Because the area gets 13 to 15 metres of snow a year and has been described by more than one Olympic champion as 'the best powder in the world.'

First-class facilities extend to more than efficient lifts, of course. Bulgaria—until recently one of the fastest up-and-coming ski destinations—has fallen from grace because many European skiers want a better *après-ski* experience than the country can offer. In fact, despite the hype by auctioneers and developers, Bulgaria is definitely not a good investment option. An over-supply of properties, lack of resale market and failure by most promoters to honour their 'guaranteed rental' promises make it risky. There is also a worryingly large disparity between the price of local and resort properties.

So where should you be looking for peak returns? The choice, purely from an investment viewpoint, divides into traditional European resorts, of which Austria, France and Switzerland offer the best value, and more exotic resorts, such as those found in Canada or Japan.

AUSTRIA
Buyers have been slow to realise that since Austria joined the European Union the restrictions limiting the amount of property sold to foreigners have been largely lifted. Some areas are easier than others. You can buy in Salzburg, for instance, provided you make the property available for rental, but it is still almost impossible to buy for holiday use in the Tirol. Prices are extremely competitive when compared with the rest of Europe. A ski-in, ski-out chalet in, say, the province of Carinthia can be had for about €175,000, whereas the same thing would probably cost about €250,000 in Salzburg. In general, decent property is about €2,000 per square metre.

FRANCE

The first thing to remember about investment property in France is that you can save a fortune if you go for a French leaseback deal. I've written about these before, and if you want extra information please e-mail or write to me. Between 2002 and 2005 areas such as Tignes and Courchevel enjoyed 25% a year capital appreciation and still managed to deliver rental yields of 4 to 5%. One of the big pluses with many French ski resorts is that they are also designed for summer holidays—optimising the rental return. A two-bedroom apartment in somewhere such as Tignes will set you back €325,000 or more; but the Pyrenees or Val d'Isère offer better value. At the bottom end you will find studio flats in somewhere such as Chamrousse from €60,000. In general, decent property is about €6,000 to €7,000 per square metre.

SWITZERLAND

The Swiss Alps are still about a third cheaper than the French Alps—but prices are catching up fast. The best investment opportunities are in the smaller, less well-known resorts, often in close proximity to larger, better-known resorts. For instance, you might consider Les Collons, which is in the same area as Verbier. Climate change is definitely an issue in the Alps, and you should buy at altitude and avoid the lower resort areas, such as Gstaad. Prices have been rising at between 15 and 20% a year, and mortgage interest rates are low.

CANADA

Capital growth in Canada has been slow to date. For instance, in three of the more popular areas—Kootenay, Blue Mountain and Tremblant—it has been running at no more than 7% a year. This is, of course, still an excellent return, but one has to remember that there is an abundance of land in Canada, and if prices rise developers tend to simply build more homes. This said, the high-altitude resorts offer a long season and luxury facilities, and rental yields have been a reliable 3 to 7% for many years. What's more, larger properties represent excellent value for money: €150,000 will buy you a nice chalet in somewhere such as Banff or Whistler.

JAPAN
Niseko in the south-west corner of Japan's northern island, Hokkaido, has been receiving a lot of positive attention from the international ski set in the last few years. Why? Because the area gets some of the best snow in the world, yet the slopes are relatively under-utilised. Prices have been climbing rapidly—33% growth was recorded last year alone—which goes against the general trend in Japan, where land prices are in their fifteenth consecutive year of decline. Still, compared with Europe or even Canada, you get a lot for your money. A six-bedroom luxury chalet, for instance, can be had for about €350,000. So keen are the local people to attract international buyers that many have been going on English-language courses, and Niseko Real Estate now has an English-language web site (www.niseko realestate.com).

Before making any financial decision you should always take professional advice.

(First published 14 January 2007)

37 | EASY DOES IT
(SLOW) REGULAR INVESTMENTS

You may have read in the media about something called the 'slow food' movement. Its supporters believe that the tastiest, most nutritious food is created slowly and carefully. I am thinking of starting a 'slow money' movement. Why? Because the best way to enjoy real, lasting wealth is to create it slowly and carefully.

What many people don't realise is that it is possible to build up a sizeable fortune simply by investing a small amount regularly. Let me give you just one example. If you started saving €10 a day on your eighteenth birthday and continued until you were sixty, assuming an average annual return of 8%, you would end up with a staggering €1,180,253. Obviously, it helps if you start saving money when you are relatively young—but it isn't vital. Follow the simple, straightforward ideas outlined below and you will find that the easiest way to get rich is . . . slowly.

Start with a little financial housekeeping. The first step to becoming a 'slow' millionaire is putting your financial house in order. There are three things you should consider. Firstly, are you wasting money that might be better used elsewhere? For example, could you save on your mortgage, cut the cost of your utilities or reduce your spending in some area? Secondly, do you have any expensive loans? There is no point in saving money that would be better used to pay off debts. Few investments earn more than it costs to borrow. Thirdly, are you budgeting properly? There is much to be said for adding up all your regular monthly outgoings, dividing by 12 and then transferring this sum into a special 'budget' account when you get paid. This should help you save cash over the course of the year.

Create a safety net. Before you focus on the more lucrative ways to make your money grow you should build up an emergency fund. The purpose of such a fund is to ensure that you have cash available to cover unexpected expenses, and ideally it should be sufficient to cover at least three months of your regular outgoings. Obviously, you need to keep it where you can get your hands on it, but that doesn't mean accepting a low return. The best option is an instant-access (or 'demand') account with a bank or credit union. At present rates vary from 0.15% a year (in other words, 15 cents for every €100 saved) to 4% (€4 for every €100 saved)—so it is worth shopping around. You will notice, by the way, that locking your money away for a period (anything from seven days to a year or more) won't necessarily increase the amount of interest you earn.

Consider a regular savings plan. With money in the bank for a rainy day, the next stage in your wealth-building plan is to start a regular savings plan. You may like to consider instalment savings with An Post. Investors save a fixed monthly instalment for twelve months, and the total amount thus saved is then invested for five years. The amount of the instalment can be between €25 and €500 a month. The guaranteed rate of return is 15% tax-free over five years from the end of the twelve-month contribution period. This is equivalent to an average annual rate of return of 2.57%, taking account of the contribution period.

An alternative is to invest in a pooled investment. Pooled investments come in many forms, with names like 'unit trusts' and 'managed funds', but they all work on the same basis. Your money—along with the money of all the other people taking part—is pooled and then invested. Each pooled investment fund has different objectives. For instance, one might invest in the largest Irish companies, another in European companies, a third in Korean property and so forth. In each case the 'fund managers'—the people running the fund and making the investment decisions—will indicate the type of risk involved. They will also provide you with regular written reports or statements explaining how your money is performing.

Pooled investments are ideal for smaller investors, but watch out for the charges that some fund managers make. Remember too that not all fund managers are good at what they do; so pick your fund carefully. Pooled investments should be thought of as medium to long-term investment vehicles. In other words, you should plan to leave your money in them for an absolute minimum of five years—and more like ten years or even longer.

Once you have built up some capital. After a few years of regular saving you will be in the happy position of having some lump sums of capital. This will open the door to bigger and better opportunities.

As the stock market has produced the highest returns over the medium to long term, it makes sense to put a large percentage of your capital into shares. You can do this by means of pooled investments or index or tracker funds (which I have written about before) or by choosing individual shares yourself. Whatever route you choose, if you mirror past performance you can look forward to some pretty juicy profits. For instance, the average return from the Irish stock market over the last ten years was 222%: in other words, every €1,000 invested in 1996 would now be worth €3,220.

Incidentally, if you'd like to dabble in the stock market but only have a relatively small amount of money to invest, why not start an investment club? An investment club is when a group of friends or colleagues pool their resources and make buy and sell decisions together. Investment clubs regularly outperform the stock market. The Irish Stock Exchange has published a booklet, *Investment Clubs: A Guide to Establishing and Running a Club for Equity Investors in Ireland*, which is available from the ISE web site (www.ise.ie) or 28 Anglesey Street, Dublin 2.

One final thought. Don't forget the benefits offered by prize bonds. These are government securities that, instead of attracting interest, participate in draws for weekly cash prizes. You can encash these bonds at any time. The amount of the prize fund is determined as a percentage of the value of the outstanding bonds, at present 2.40% per annum, and the winnings are 100% tax-free. You can invest as little as €25, and the largest monthly prize is €150,000.

Before making any financial decision you should always take professional advice.

(First published 7 January 2007)

38 | HIDEAWAY IN THE SUN
SPANISH PROPERTY

If you can get your hands on €32,000 to €100,000 over the next few months and you wouldn't say no to the idea of doubling or even trebling your money in a relatively short period (and with fairly low risk), then I have two words to say to you: Medina Elvira. In the heart of Andalucía, with its miles and miles of olive trees, only minutes from the famous Arab palace of Alhambra, this luxury development has everything going for it.

Spain, and especially well-chosen Spanish property, offers plenty of potential for profit. Twenty years ago the country was beset by labour problems and the economy was highly dependent on farming, low-cost manufacturing and budget tourism. Today, however, business is booming and the gross domestic product (GDP) is growing at close to 4% a year, compared with a European average of 2.7%.

Property prices have reflected this growth, and yet—because they were so low to begin with—there is still plenty of value to be found. In plain English, your euro buys you considerably more in Spain than it does here at home. Speaking of which, the fact that Spain is in the euro zone is another important benefit, as it removes any currency risk.

True, the country's current-account deficit is the highest in the developed world, running at 7.3% of GDP, compared with, say, 5.8% in the United States. Nevertheless, all the indicators are that the economy will continue to expand, and—more pertinently—some 10 million more people are expected to buy property in Spain over the next decade.

You may have noticed widely diverging media reports about the Spanish property market. Some claim that the huge growth experienced since the late 1990s (currently 15.6% a year) is likely to continue for some time; others suggest that there is a glut of buy-to-let property on the market and that prices have levelled off and may even fall. Both statements are true. First-rate properties in first-rate areas are in high demand and there is every reason to expect long-term growth. Europe's changing demographics, the population shift to the south and the fact that prices compare favourably with other similar places all reinforce this view. The demand for second-rate properties in second-rate areas, however, has almost definitely reached a plateau.

I base this on personal observation. Last year I visited Spain half a dozen times in order to thoroughly research the market. I won't pretend that having to make regular business trips to Spain was a hardship. I love the life-style, the people, the culture, the food and the wine. Oh, and the sports. The secret is to get away from the over-rated, overdeveloped and overhyped areas and to immerse oneself in the real Spain. Granada has long been a favourite destination—steeped in history, surrounded by stunning countryside and packed with things to see and do.

It is convenient to get to—it has its own airport, or you can fly to Málaga—yet it remains delightfully unspoiled. Drive for half an hour in one direction and you can be skiing in the Sierra Nevada mountains; drive forty minutes in the other and you can be lounging on the beach. No wonder developers choose it for their latest, upmarket developments! Medina Elvira is beside Lake Cubillas (excellent fishing, swimming and boating) and built around an eighteen-hole championship golf course managed by Sotogrande (the Valderrama people). Perhaps more to the point, the figures stack up.

The essential issue with an overseas property investment is that even if you decide to use it a bit yourself you want it to be largely self-financing. Most developers nowadays offer guaranteed rental income. The important thing is to judge whether the relevant parties are (*a*) well established, (*b*) bonded and (*c*) reliable. In the case of Medina Elvira the guarantee is realistic: 5% a year for ten years. Better still, the guarantee comes from tour operators, so it is definitely bonded. What's more, it is possible to buy off plan with only a deposit of 10%. After twelve months you pay a further 10% and on completion, twenty-four months later, you pay the 80% balance.

Prices range from €160,000 to €500,000, with a typical two-bedroom apartment adjoining the golf course (including club membership—you could sell this on at €10,000) costing about €315,000. Mortgages of 80% are available, and if prices continue to rise at the current rate one could potentially mortgage at 100% on completion at the end of two years.

Supposing you buy at the bottom end. You would need €16,000 now and €16,000 in a year and could then take out a minimum mortgage of €128,000. At today's rates of 4.75% the monthly interest-only payments would be €506—but the guaranteed monthly rental income would be €500, and this after the 25% tax on rental income has been paid over to the Spanish government. Obviously, one is hoping for a capital gain. If prices continue to rise at 15.6% for the next five years your €160,000 property would be worth a minimum of €330,300—not bad for an initial outlay of €32,000.

Finally, I want to make a couple of ethical points. Every time I write one of these articles I am putting my own reputation as a financial adviser on the line. I must, therefore, make it absolutely clear that an investment like this is definitely not for everyone. If you haven't got substantial other assets—property in Ireland or shares, for instance—you shouldn't be considering this sort of diversification. Furthermore, you should always take professional advice before making any major financial decision.

Also, I need to declare a vested interest. Like Victor Kiam (if you are as old as I am you may remember he was so convinced Remington made a better electric razor that he bought the company), I was so convinced by Medina Elvira that I negotiated to act as one of their authorised agents, and I will definitely be buying a property there myself. This means, of course, that if you contact me I will be only too pleased to let you have more information and arrange a visit. It also means that we may well become neighbours!

(First published 28 January 2007)

39 | HI-YO, SILVER!
SILVER

'I was just trying to make some money,' Nelson Bunker Hunt reputedly said when explaining to his sister how he lost an estimated $1 billion trying to corner the silver market in 1979. Ever since 'Silver Thursday', 27 March 1980, when the price tumbled from $21.62 down to $10.80 per ounce, bankrupting the Hunt family in the process, the precious metal's reputation has been somewhat tarnished.

Yet over the last few years silver has been steadily climbing in price. In 2006, for instance, the price fluctuated between $9.25 and $12.70 per ounce—substantially higher than its twenty-year average, which has mainly been in the $3–$8 range. Indeed, if you had put €1,000 into silver at the end of 2001 (when the price was about $4.70 per ounce) and had sold at the end of 2006 (when the price was about $12.70 per ounce) you would have made €2,702, or 270%, profit. What's more, there are plenty of reasons to believe that the trend is going to continue upwards—possibly at a much faster pace—making it an ideal choice for anyone wishing to invest in a solid alternative asset.

The strongest argument for putting money into silver is irrefutable: for the last fifteen years or so demand has consistently outstripped supply. Silver is used in a vast array of industrial applications. It conducts electricity better than any other metal, doesn't corrode, is extremely sensitive to light and has anti-bacterial properties. As a result it is used in everything from jet-engine lubricants to battery cathodes and from purifying water to photographic development. (The launch of digital photography, incidentally, has had only a minimal effect on the market.) Silver is also used in making jewellery and silverware for the home. So, as one would expect, with growing worldwide industrialisation and development, demand has been growing.

Why hasn't supply kept up? The price of silver was in the doldrums for such a long period that mine-owners did not invest in production. It takes years to get a mine up and running, and the risks are high. Anyway, the deficit has been met from existing stockpiles, especially government-owned sources. These, however, have now been run down. In 1990 there were 2.2 billion ounces of silver held in above-ground stocks. Last year there were probably about 300 million ounces. Not to put too fine a point on it, silver stocks are at a fifty-year low, a low that may eventually be cured by increased production but that in the short to medium term many believe will result in huge price rises.

If the thought of silver shortages doesn't convince you, a look at the relative prices of gold and silver may. Over the last 350 years the ratio between silver and gold has been 30:1. In other words, since about 1650 you have needed an average of 30 ounces of silver to buy a single ounce of gold. At the moment you need about 50 ounces of silver to buy a single ounce of gold. In theory, the price of silver—relative to gold—should double to attain its historic average.

The theory of investing in silver and the practice are two completely different things. This is best illustrated by the comparative weights of various precious metals. If you buy $50,000 of platinum it will weigh approximately 45 oz (slightly less than 3 lb); the same value of gold will weigh approximately 79 oz (nearly 5 lb); but the same value of silver will weigh approximately 17 stone 5 lb! Storing more than a relatively low value of silver is clearly impractical, which is why many investors turn to the publicly quoted stocks as a way into the market.

Unfortunately, the most productive silver mines are owned by larger, diversified mining groups, meaning that you are really buying into the whole mining sector rather than silver itself. Bear in mind too that less than a third of silver produced each year comes from silver mines: the rest is a by-product of other mining activities. If you buy into the biggest silver-miner in the world, for instance, BHP Billiton, you are exposed to a range of commodities, including diamonds, coal, zinc, oil and gas; Kazakhmys, another huge silver producer, is better known for its copper mining; while Rio Tinto, again in the top ten silver producers, is into everything from salt to uranium. There are a number of pure silver-miners, but they are mostly in the United States. You will see that the two major players are Pan-American Silver and Silver Standard.

One thing to study is each mining company's production costs. For instance, a firm called Heela Mining produces silver at about $2 per ounce—meaning that it must be enjoying healthy profits right now.

Another possibility is to buy into the Barclay Bank Silver Trust, which is an exchange-traded fund (ETF), listed in the United States. ETFs—pooled investments—hold physical commodities on behalf of their clients and are best known for the effect they have had on gold and other markets. I have written about them before so I will say only that if you are interested in knowing more please e-mail me. The main benefit of any ETF is that it gives you direct exposure to the market without any of the usual complications (security, sales tax and so forth), and you can buy and sell quickly and relatively inexpensively.

Finally, you could consider buying antique silver items. These can prove to be excellent investments, as they are sometimes sold at non-specialist auctions for little more than the value of the melted-down metal. On the plus side, if silver doesn't rise by as much as you hope, you will still have a valuable and usable antique.

Obviously, silver is an alternative investment, and you shouldn't consider it unless you already own other assets, such as property and shares. Note that the price over the short term can be highly volatile. Incidentally, if you 'Google' for information about investing in silver you will find dozens of crank sites. Some of the slightly more conservative commentators include www.silver-investor.com, www.silverseek.com and www.silverstock report.com. You can also access a live silver price quote from www.kitco.com/charts/livesilver.html, while a useful Irish site is www.gold.ie, which specialises in all the precious metals.

Remember, you should always take professional advice before making any financial decision.

(First published 4 February 2007)

40 | HIGHER EDUCATION
SECTION 50 PROPERTY

You probably think of students as being boisterous, messy and disorganised, but if you were letting property to them you might think otherwise. Because if there is one class of tenant that consistently produces higher yields it is third-level students—not just here in Ireland but overseas as well. So, if you have always dreamt of building up a portfolio of properties that would produce sufficiently high income to cover the cost of your borrowing while simultaneously offering the potential of substantial capital gains, this could be the sector to specialise in.

Before looking at some of the different options let's consider why students make such profitable tenants. To begin with, they are easy to find and easy to keep. Once you have a tenant for the academic year they are unlikely to move elsewhere. What's more, there is no reason why—if you buy in the right location—your property should remain vacant during the summer holidays. In many cities there is strong demand for short lettings. Even if there isn't, you should be able to charge above the going rate in order to compensate you for the void periods. Incidentally, students will frequently accept a lower, more crowded standard of accommodation. They would rather pay less rent than have a luxury bathroom or even a sitting-room.

Students are good payers too. Some will have their rent underwritten by their parents or guardians, and others may agree to pay an entire year's rent in advance. Either way, you can demand cast-iron guarantees and relax in the knowledge that you are unlikely to be affected by many of the problems that face most landlords, such as tenants who become unemployed or stop paying their rent.

Not that there aren't downsides. In general, student lettings incur slightly higher upkeep charges. They are, to put it politely, somewhat more accident-prone and less likely to undertake non-essential maintenance.

The secret to successful student letting is to research the market carefully. Some university towns have a surplus of beds, others a shortage. By buying property in places that are also home to young professionals or seasonal visitors you can be doubly certain of never being without a tenant. You may also find that relatively modest investments in such facilities as broadband access and simple shower rooms *en suite* will help to improve your returns.

Where should you buy? There are definitely opportunities in Ireland—but you would be wise to consider looking overseas as well. Britain has the advantage of being our nearest neighbour, with 2.3 million students in higher education. The United States, with more than 9½ million students, offers unusually high yields and extra value because of the weak dollar. One thing is certain: world student numbers are rising, by up to 5% a year and more, in the developed countries. As only a tiny percentage of these students will ever buy their own property—and as colleges rarely move—you will be investing in a growing, secure market.

Ireland. In general, the situation for Irish landlords with residential property is improving. At the end of 2006, according to Daft.ie, rents throughout the country had grown, in year-on-year terms, by an average of 10.1%— marking twenty-four months of consecutive growth. What's more, property is only staying vacant for an average of nine days between tenants—a clear indication that demand is strong. Average yields, however, are still relatively low, which means that you have to buy carefully if you are going to enjoy sufficient return on your income to service, say, a 90% mortgage. On the whole, you are likely to enjoy a substantially higher yield if you buy outside Dublin.

Let me give you just one example. A client of mine recently found a four-bedroom property in Glasnevin on the north side of Dublin that could be converted to accommodate six students. The cost, including an allowance for building work and furniture, was €550,000, and the anticipated annual rent would be €42,000—an initial yield of 7.63%. If you borrowed 90% of the final valuation and purchase price on an interest-only basis your annual payments at an interest rate of 4.75% would be €23,512. If house prices continued to increase at the same level for the next twenty years, as they have for the last twenty years, you would enjoy a substantial gain. Even if they were to grow at a very modest 6% a year—as forecast by Nib's 20/20 Vision (the next fourteen years)— compounded, you would still double your money every twelve years.

In Ireland we also have the added incentive of section 50 relief. This is a tax relief brought in by the Government to encourage investment in student accommodation. Simply, it means that if you buy a designated student accommodation property—there are still many such developments available around the country—as much as 90% of the cost of the property can be offset not only against your rental income tax liability of the student property bought but also against *all* rental income tax liability. Ideal for portfolio investors. E-mail me for further information on this tax relief.

United States. The magazine *Forbes* has just highlighted student apartment complexes as being one of the hottest investment opportunities for 2007 and beyond. Why? Because the yields—net rental income (rent minus property taxes and other operating costs) divided by property value—have been running at a steady 6 to 7% a year, compared with, say, Manhattan office space at around 5½%. More to the point, 70% of students live outside college, while total numbers are still growing (up 20% in the last decade) and won't peak until 2010 at the soonest.

You can get into the market by buying shares in an equity real-estate investment trust (REIT)—basically managed funds that specialise in this sector—though you need to choose your trust carefully. Names to consider include American Campus Communities, Home Properties and Mid-America Apartment Communities. Alternatively, you could buy individual properties direct. Either way, a weak dollar is going to work in your favour.

Britain. Last year the *Financial Times* reported that yields on student lettings can be as high as 10%, compared with an average of about 5% for buy-to-let generally. Halifax, one of Britain's leading mortgage providers, recently found that the top twenty student locations have seen average property rises of 77% over the past five years— two facts that suggest that letting to British students will produce high returns and capital gains. Personally, I would look at those student locations where property is still trading at a discount to the surrounding area. In the same Halifax survey I note that they discovered that property in five top university areas—Bristol, Birmingham, Nottingham, London (King's College) and Coventry—cost less.

Remember, you should always take professional advice before making any financial decision.

(First published 15 April 2007)

41 | READY FOR A CLOSE-UP?
FILM INVESTMENT

A re you a big fan of the silver screen? Do you have some spare cash—as little as €8,414—that you want to invest? Would you like to reduce your annual income-tax bill? If you can answer 'yes' to all these questions then you may like to consider an alternative investment that is becoming increasingly mainstream: backing a film or television production.

The lure of the big (or, increasingly nowadays, the little) screen is easy to understand. With good research and professional advice you should be able to achieve above-average returns. And, if you are lucky, you may manage to fund a huge hit that could bring you in a capital gain as well as a regular income for years. Not that all the benefits of film investment are financial. As one of the angels you may be asked to appear in the production (some of the best lines in *Four Weddings and a Funeral* were delivered by those who financed it), and you can definitely expect to be invited to meet the stars and attend one of the premieres.

It is a big mistake to ever make an investment because of the available tax relief. If an investment doesn't stack up on its own, it should be avoided. Nevertheless, the tax breaks enjoyed by those who put money into films are very attractive. This is because as long ago as 1984 the Government decided to support the film industry by means of tax concessions for private investors. The nature of this relief has changed over the years. First it was through BES, then something called section 35. Nowadays it is governed by section 481 of the Taxes Consolidation Act (1997). The rules pertaining to section 481 are complicated, but in essence:

- Tax relief can be available for films, television drama, creative documentaries and animation.
- The Revenue Commissioners grant the relief in advance, so the tax breaks are guaranteed before you invest.
- Relief is claimed at your marginal rate of tax.
- Relief is available for 80% of the amount invested in the film.
- The maximum amount you can invest in any one year is €31,750—though you may need as little as €8,414 in cash to take advantage of the relief.
- The holding period for the relief from capital gains tax is just one year.

Most film investors take advantage of the section 481 relief through a managed investment scheme. How does this work? Typically, you would subscribe for €31,750 of shares in a film, of which 26% would be in cash (i.e. the €8,414) and the rest in the form of a pre-arranged loan, generally through a bank; Anglo-Irish Bank PLC would be the leaders in this area. After the agreed period—usually within a year—the tax rebate is sent back to your bank. Assuming you pay tax at the top rate of 41% and you have invested €31,750, then the 80% that is allowable for relief (€25,400) would be worth €10,414 to you by way of that rebate. Anglo-Irish Bank, meanwhile, has secured money from the producer of the film to cover the 74% loan and accrued interest through an agreement called the Defeasan Arrangement.

Therefore, at no risk you finish up with a tax-free payment of €2,000, equivalent to 23.77% return on your investment—not a bad return when compared with, say, leaving your cash on deposit with a bank, which is unlikely to pay you more than 4% a year.

The sort of managed investment scheme I have just described is readily available through a number of financial institutions, including Anglo-Irish Bank and Allied Irish Bank. Indeed last year AIB raised finance for dozens of different film projects, including €21 million for *The Tudors*, and now claims to be the largest provider of section 481 funding in the country. The upside of these schemes is relatively low risk, given the nature of films and television. The downside is that returns will be limited.

If you are willing to tolerate a much higher risk in exchange for a much higher potential return then you need to look for more direct investment in a low-budget or independent production. If you are canny you could back a cult film, such as *Clerks* ($8 million gross income on a budget of $50,000), *The Brothers McCullen* ($10 million gross income on a budget of $50,000) or *Chasing Amy* ($12 million gross income on a budget of $500,000).

How do you find worthwhile opportunities, and, having found them, how do you judge the potential? Happily, the Irish film industry is booming. As a result there is no shortage of international talent—writers, directors and producers—living on these shores. The first step for anyone thinking of putting cash into anything other than a professionally managed investment scheme is to familiarise himself or herself with what's going on. There are plenty of places to look, including:

- Irish Film and Television Network (www.iftn.ie)
- Screen Producers Ireland (www.screenproducers ireland.com)
- Irish Film Board (www.irishfilmboard.ie)
- *Film Ireland* (www.filmireland.net)
- Screen Directors Guild of Ireland (www.sdgi.ie)
- Northern Ireland Film and Television Commission (www.niftc.co.uk).

I particularly recommend *Film Ireland*, which carries extensive coverage in the form of news, special reports, interviews and reviews.

Having begun to get an idea of what is going on, you need to decide how much you wish to invest and what sort of production you are interested in backing. Here are some tips:

- Make sure that section 481 relief is going to be available to you, and work out what it is going to be worth in cash terms.
- Don't write anyone a cheque without a formal agreement or a contract. Make sure your money will be returned to you if the production doesn't go ahead.
- Learn how film financing works. There are some good books on the subject. I found *The Insider's Guide to Film Finance* by Philip Alberstat very useful—but there are dozens to choose from. You need to be familiar with all the terminology.
- Look closely at the budget. Who is getting paid what?
- Consider the record of all those involved. The more experience they have, the greater your chance of hitting the jackpot.

Whether you opt for a managed investment scheme or something with a much higher degree of risk attached to it, one thing is certain: backing a film will bring you lots of interesting 'action', but it's not for the faint-hearted.

Remember, you should always take professional advice before making any financial decision, especially in this area of investment.

(First published 18 February 2007)

42 | GLAD TO BE GREY
PENSION SCHEMES

Sir Thomas Beecham, the conductor, famously chided a cello player in the following terms: 'Madam, you have between your legs one of the most beautiful instruments in the world and yet all you can do is scratch at it.'

It is the same story when it comes to the Irish pension system. We enjoy, without question, the most beautiful pension system in the world and yet what do most people do? They barely even scratch at it. The reason is, of course, that almost everything that is ever written or said about pensions tends to be unnecessarily technical and, frankly, boring. If only those responsible for encouraging people to take advantage of the pension system sexed it up a bit. There is nothing dull, after all, about turning every 59 cents you invest into €1 in the time it takes you to sign your name, or being able to shield your entire annual salary— and more besides—from income tax for years on end, or passing your pension fund on to your children tax-free, to offer just three examples. And there certainly isn't anything boring about being able to retire young and rich. The fact is, everyone should be encouraged to see pension planning not as a tedious chore but as the hottest, most lucrative money-making opportunity in the country.

Ironically, the reason why putting your money into a pension is the best investment you can make is because so few people actually do so.

The national reluctance to save for retirement has worried successive Governments to such an extent that they have introduced ludicrously generous incentives in order to motivate us to take action. These incentives come in the form of (*a*) extraordinarily high tax breaks and (*b*) extremely flexible rules.

Before you start to glaze over, let me just point out that the real effect of not paying tax on money you put into (or make from) a pension fund means that the underlying investment doesn't have to perform terribly well for you to be earning a small fortune, while the real effect of the flexible rules means that your pension fund can do all sorts of things, like borrowing extra cash to buy, say, a property and thus further boost your profits.

But let's not get bogged down in pension rules. The main thing is, how much money can you make for yourself by starting or adding to a retirement plan? As the answer will depend on all sorts of factors, such as your employment status and age, I think the best way to answer this is to cite a couple of actual case histories taken from my client files.

The first is of a single senior executive who, as a PAYE employee, took out a pension plan with a major insurance company at the age of fifty. As he pays tax at the top rate of 41%, every euro he puts into the pension scheme only costs him 59 cents. In other words, before the money is actually invested it has almost doubled in value. What's more, when he reaches the age of fifty-five he can avail of the new higher thresholds: 35% of your income for the over-55s can be put away in a pension and 40% for over-60s. He earned just over €100,000 in 2005/06, so last year he was able to invest 30%, or €30,000, in his pension. While he started late, he can still look forward to a pension fund of €1,118,000 at sixty-five, based on a 6% growth rate for the next fifteen years. Apart from a tax-free lump sum on retirement of 25% of the fund (i.e. €279,500), he can look forward to an annual pension of €55,428 for the rest of his life.

The second case history is of a company owner-director, aged forty-three, who set up a small self-administered pension scheme or self-directed trust. The company pays into this scheme on his behalf and saves on corporation tax, so he can't claim tax relief. However, his pension scheme is (under recent legislation) able to borrow money to buy property. There are four main benefits to this:

- The loan repayments are considered pension contributions and therefore tax-free (normally when repaying loans you have to earn money, pay tax and then make a payment from the surplus).
- There is no tax on the rental income, because it stays in the trust (further reducing the amount borrowed).
- There is no capital gains tax either when the property is sold, because it is within a pension.
- Finally, you can pass the trust on to your family after your death.

How does this work in practice? Although this particular client draws an income of €100,000, the rules allow his company to pay up to 160% of his annual income into his trust. In fact it decided to pay €150,000 a year into his trust.

The trust then invested in a buy-to-let apartment for €500,000, borrowing 70% or €350,000 over fifteen years, with the balance being the first year's contribution. Rental income from the property was €1,400 a month, while the capital and interest payments were €2,722.41 per month.

With service charges of approximately €100 per month, the annual shortfall was exactly €30,268. As the client's company is making an annual tax-free contribution of €150,000, the trust will be able to repay the loan in just over two years. Remember, all the income and capital gains generated by the property are also tax-free.

As you might expect, there are a number of restrictions with these trusts (one is that you cannot put your home, office or any other properties you already own into the trust), and your authorised adviser can give you the low-down or you can contact me for further information. For sole traders, a new type of trust, called self-invested personal pensions (sipps), is now available through three insurance companies, with roughly the same parameters as self-directed trusts. Again, please do contact me for details.

I've been trying to sell you on the idea of pension planning on investment grounds, but if you aren't persuaded by greed then maybe you will be persuaded by fear. We are living longer, and we stop work (not always voluntarily) earlier, with the result that it is not unusual to spend the last twenty years or more of our lives in retirement. The present maximum single person's weekly pension is—wait for it—€200 a week. And that's the maximum! If you haven't reviewed your pension recently, even if you are looking forward to a pension through your employer, for goodness' sake seek out professional help.

Remember, you should always take professional advice before making any financial decision.

(First published 4 March 2007)

43 | THE WAGES OF SIN
INVESTING IN HUMAN WEAKNESS

The Devil has the best tunes, and he also, as it happens, has some of the best investments. Because if you are interested in making money it is hard to beat the returns offered by companies that take advantage of humankind's failings. For my own part I subscribe firmly to the idea of socially responsible investment. However, from a financial viewpoint there can be no doubt that vice is not just nice: it's lucrative.

Tobacco, gambling, alcohol and armaments—to name the principal sectors—have always shown consistent, above-average returns. Why should this be? Whatever different governments and societies may ordain, the fact is that vice, in all its many guises, never seems to go out of fashion. Indeed, whether markets rise or fall, wars will be waged and people will seek comfort in such things as smoking, drinking and a flutter on the horses. Vice stocks are—like it or not—essentially recession-proof, leading many investors to hold them as a defensive play against a possible slowdown in economic growth.

There is only one managed fund specialising in

gambling, tobacco, alcohol and defence-related stocks. It is called, appropriately enough, the Vice Fund, and it was launched in the United States in 2002. Since then it has outpaced the Standard and Poor (S&P) 500 Index by 23%, delivering gains of just over 18% a year. Charles Norton, the man who manages the fund, describes himself as 'a conservative family man' and stresses that he likes to invest in vice stocks because they are 'very strong' performers.

It would be a mistake, though, to think that all vice stocks are equal. To achieve such gains regularly requires an active investment strategy that takes into account both sector developments and individual company prospects. Here is a quick round-up of the different options.

1. Light up your portfolio. Smokers in the First World may be quitting, and countries may be leaping on the public ban bandwagon, but the tobacco sector is still thriving. Why? Sales in emerging markets are growing, costs are being slashed by moving manufacturing to the Far East and eastern Europe, and there is the prospect that sooner or later the Chinese market—the Chinese smoke two trillion cigarettes a year—will eventually be opened to foreign competition. Giants such as British American Tobacco, Imperial Tobacco or SAB Miller seem set to prosper for the foreseeable future.

2. A sure bet. The gaming industry has been dominated over the last few years by the rise of on-line gambling. There are about 2,500 gaming web sites, generating an estimated €9 to €10 billion a year. However, when the US government decided to crack down on on-line gambling— it is illegal to offer it to US residents—the whole sector took a hit. The result is that many stocks, especially those that weren't particularly exposed to the US market, could offer value.

Some of the larger British players look especially

attractive, as the government there has deregulated the gaming industry in a bid to compete with tourist destinations such as Las Vegas. You might also consider backing one of the companies operating in Macau, where gaming revenues are growing by more than 40% a year; take a look at Wynn Resorts or Melco International Development, for instance.

3. A drink to celebrate. The drinks industry has been going through a period of change. Some sectors—most noticeably pubs and bars, which have been hit by smoking or proposed smoking bans, not just here in Ireland but overseas as well—are having a tough time. Brewers are suffering too, as more people (especially in the United States) are turning away from beer to other tipples.

Distillers and vintners, on the other hand, have been enjoying steady growth, as have some distribution companies. One company I have seen tipped in several places is the American giant AmBev; another, at the opposite end of the scale, is Central European Distribution. The latter is Poland's largest vodka producer and makes me wonder if the biggest gains might come from emerging markets. On the home front, c&c have had a sparkling twelve months.

4. Aerospace and defence. As the *Financial Times* recently commented, 'defence stocks represent a particularly good deal given the amount governments allocate to funding wars. In 2006 defence stocks outperformed the s&p 500 for the sixth time in the last seven years.' For those who feel squeamish about armaments, the closely linked aerospace industry offers a more morally acceptable alternative. Two companies that have performed consistently over the last three decades are Lockheed Martin and General Dynamics.

5. Making money from 'it'. I don't like to mention the 's' word in a family newspaper, but without involving yourself in anything even remotely tacky there are ways to profit from 'it'. Consider, for instance, investing in one of the growing number of firms that offer specialist pharmaceutical products, such as Pfizer, Eli Lilly or Berlex; or one of the companies running fertility clinics; or maybe even manufacturers of a well-known brand starting with the letter 'D'—SSL International PLC—or one of their competitors.

If you are interested in investing in vice stocks, then either you will need to do a considerable amount of detailed research or ask a broker to assist you. Whichever route you opt for I would recommend visiting some of the different on-line bulletin boards providing forums for shareholders to exchange information and ideas. One that I recommend is ADVFN (www.advfn.com), another is the Motley Fool (www.fool.com). If you are keen to learn more about the Vice Fund I mentioned above, its web site is www.vicefund.com. The minimum investment is $4,000 (just over €3,000), but do bear in mind that this is a relatively high-risk fund and that you will be exposed to any fluctuation in the exchange rate between the euro and the US dollar.

Remember, you should always take professional advice before making any financial decision.

(First published 25 February 2007)

44 | THE NAME GAME
LLOYD'S SYNDICATES

Not everyone is unhappy when the cost of insurance goes up. One group in particular are positively delighted. These are the people who have had the perspicacity to put some of their cash into one of the least-understood, but potentially most profitable, investments ever devised: underwriting insurance.

For private investors the easiest and most lucrative way to do this is to get involved with the best-known insurance market in the world: Lloyd's of London. Once upon a time this meant becoming a 'Name'—one of the incredibly wealthy individuals who pocket a large percentage of the insurance premiums in exchange for shouldering some of the risk. Now, although becoming a Name happens to be an increasingly attractive option for the super-rich, there are plenty of other ways to make money from Lloyd's. Returns of up to 35% a year are not impossible, and you could actually participate, albeit indirectly, with a few hundred euros.

In the seventeenth century Edward Lloyd's coffee-house in Tower Street, London, was popular with sailors, merchants and shipowners. He provided them not only with refreshment but also with extremely accurate shipping news, and as a result the establishment evolved into a meeting-place for those involved in the fledgling marine insurance business.

Since then Lloyd's has undergone many reincarnations, but its main purpose remains unchanged. It's a market. Like any market, it enables those with something to sell—underwriters providing insurance coverage—to make contact with those who want to buy—brokers working on behalf of their clients who are seeking insurance. For instance, a broker working for a company responsible for putting telecommunications satellites into space might visit the Lloyd's building in London and 'shop around' for protection against a number of different eventualities, from the launch failing to the equipment not functioning once in orbit. He or she would visit the different syndicates 'selling' this type of insurance underwriting in search of the best price, terms and conditions. The winning syndicate's members—the Names—would have to meet the cost in the event of a claim. However, in the event of no claim they would get to keep the premiums.

This may all sound somewhat abstract, so let me put it into context. Lloyd's covers a vast range of risks, from oil rigs to—believe it or not—celebrity body parts and from major airlines to sporting events. Last year the sixty-six syndicates that make up the market did an estimated €22 billion of business. Not surprisingly, when you think of the sheer volume of money involved, a lot of people are earning huge profits, thank you very much, out of Lloyd's. Which is why I am suggesting that you consider joining them.

If you have in the region of €150,000 in cash and further available assets (for instance buy-to-let property or publicly quoted shares) of around €500,000—or if you know a group of investors with whom you could club together to raise these amounts—then you could become a member of a syndicate—in other words, a Name.

Once upon a time this would have meant unlimited liability—you may remember the terrible losses incurred by Names in the late 1980s and early 90s—but nowadays you can limit your liability to the total amount of your investment. So the maximum you can lose on a €650,000 investment is €650,000. This might not sound attractive until I explain two important things:

- Firstly, some syndicates make up to 50% profit a year.
- Secondly, Names only have to supply a percentage of their investment in cash: the rest can remain invested in other assets of their choice.

This latter point means that you can earn a return from the same capital twice: once through Lloyd's, once from some other investment. If you think this sounds good, wait until I tell you the best bit of all. When you take a minimum underwriting stake of about €450,000 it will cost you €100,000 cash up front, the balance in other assets; but you'll actually be underwriting roughly €1 million worth of premiums. Your profits or losses will be determined in relation to the €1 million. So, if the syndicate makes a 20% loss in a particular year you will have to fork out an additional €100,000; but if the syndicate makes a 20% profit your share will be €200,000. Names would expect a minimum return of 20% per annum.

Your maximum downside, according to the new guidelines—which forbid new members from accepting unlimited liability—would be a loss of £450,000 for that year; although one mild comfort is that any losses could be offset against your income-tax bill.

Other reports mention slightly different figures. If you are underwriting motor, for instance, where the risk tends to be constant from year to year, the amount of cash required is much less than if you are underwriting something of a much higher risk, such as tobacco litigation or satellites, for example.

As you might expect, investing in an underwriting stake is complicated. Syndicates are re-formed every year, and, as claims can take a long time to agree and process, they don't pay out to Names until three years have passed. Your investment can be structured as either a limited liability partnership or a limited liability company, depending on your needs. Also, you can pool resources and invest with others.

The better syndicates are difficult to join—some places are even auctioned—and it is important to remember that performances vary enormously. In general, the best way to assess what is happening in the market is to look at premium rates. When rates are low or falling, syndicates tend to lose money. When they are rising—even if there are a lot of claims—the opposite is true. It is also worth noting that the insurance market tends to perform better when the equity markets are doing badly.

The equity markets offer an interesting alternative to becoming a Name. You could, of course, invest in any publicly quoted insurance company. You could also invest in a managed fund specialising in financial institutions. However, if you would like to be more directly involved then you could buy shares in one or more of the British quoted underwriting companies. I am not in the business of 'tipping', but among the options you might care to look at are Heritage Underwriting, Kiln PLC and Omega Underwriting—the last of which was the first Lloyd's of London insurance company to list on the Alternative Investment Market.

If you have €75,000 then you could also invest in a portfolio of syndicates through Insurance Capital Partners, a managed fund run by a firm called CBS Private Capital (www.cbs-lloyds.co.uk). It is hoping to achieve a return of between 30 and 35% a year.

To learn more about making money from Lloyd's of London visit its web site: www.lloyds.com. Note that three syndicates that have performed well in recent years are Hiscox syndicate 33, Kiln syndicate 510 and Cathedral syndicate 2010. A great deal of further information is to be found on the web site of the Association of Lloyd's Members (www.alm.ltd.uk).

Remember, you should always take professional advice before making any financial decision.

(First published 29 April 2007)

45 | EXPOSE YOURSELF
EXCHANGE-TRADED FUNDS

W hat I am about to describe is an investment wolf dressed in sheep's clothing. Indeed to most people it appears to be exactly the sort of investment that one might think about if one was having a little trouble sleeping. To dismiss exchange-traded funds (ETFS) as a soporific, however, is a bad mistake for anyone dreaming of big profits. Because when it comes to a simple, easy, inexpensive method of making your money grow you would be hard pressed to find a better option.

Let's start by considering some of the problems and dilemmas every private investor faces. To begin with, there is the overriding need to diversify. Depending on your objectives, you want your money spread across a range of investments, so that whatever happens to interest rates, the economy or the markets your returns are secure. Achieving this if you have a limited amount of money is difficult, because you can't get much of a spread. After all, you need a pretty large amount of capital to diversify properly into, say, property, bonds, commodities, cash and shares.

Speaking of shares, the next issue for any investor is how best to benefit from the stock market. Over the medium to long term it is the stock market that produces the most secure returns. Whether you choose the Irish market—which has seen an average 17.4% a year growth over the last thirty-plus years—or other, international markets, it is publicly quoted shares that are most likely to provide you with consistent gains.

The third question you face is that of cost. Whether you are investing in property or buying units in a managed fund, the expenses can be surprisingly high and will eat into your profits. This is particularly true if you are trying to create a portfolio of shares that reflects a particular sector or market. Finally, liquidity has to be considered. Many of the best investments may require time (and effort) to sell.

How, then, can ETFs help? An ETF is nothing more than a basket of assets in a particular market or sector. For instance, it might be a basket of shares in Ireland's top twenty companies or the leading American commercial property firm. Its purpose is to reflect, as closely as possible, the behaviour of the index, region, country or sector that it represents. 'Aha!' I expect you are saying to yourself. 'An ETF is just a fancy name for a tracker fund.' Well, it is exactly like a tracker fund in that it should give you the same return as the chosen asset class. But there the resemblance ends; because ETFs have the following unique properties:

- They are actually listed on major stock exchanges around the world. This means you can buy and sell shares in an ETF in the same way as you would in an individual company.
- They are considerably cheaper to buy. There are no up-front charges or annual management fees. A typical managed fund might cost you 3% to buy into and between 1% and 1.5% a year in management fees. A typical ETF will cost you around 0.33% (that's a third of a cent for every €100 invested) to buy and about 0.50%

(that's less than a half of 1%) by way of total expenses ratio (TER). This covers all the expenses of the fund: administrator fees, management fees, custodian fees, amortised fees etc. Some TERS can be as low as 0.07% (such as QQQ, one of the biggest traded shares in the world, because it has billions of dollars in assets under management).

- They are easy to buy and sell. ETF prices are quoted continuously, allowing investors to buy and sell throughout the trading day.
- They are totally transparent. You always know exactly what the underlying assets are, and these details are disclosed daily.
- They are secure. ETFS are securities certificates that state the legal right of ownership over part of the fund's actual assets. In other words, you own the actual assets yourself.
- They can produce an income. Many share-based ETFS pass the dividends they receive on to their investors. Investing in an ETF need not mean just capital gain: it can mean an income stream too.

Investing in exchange-traded funds means you can buy actual commodities, such as oil and gold, without ever taking delivery of oil or carrying an ounce of gold. In fact name a sector or market and there is bound to be an ETF— or choice of ETFS—covering it.

So, what about performance? Obviously, this mirrors the performance of the underlying assets. If, for instance, you had bought into an ETF run by Barclays called iShares FTSE/Xinhua China Index, which reflects the growth of the leading Chinese public companies, about a year ago you would have enjoyed a return of more than 45%. Looking at a different sector, if at the same time you had bought into an ETF called Vanguard REIT Index ETF, which holds property, you would have enjoyed a return of more than 35%. Which brings me to another fantastic benefit of investing in ETFs: they allow you to buy into a whole class of assets in one easy step.

The ability to invest in an entire class of assets, rather than having to select individual assets, reduces risk and boosts returns. It also puts small private investors on a level playing-field with much wealthier investors, because it allows them to develop and control a portfolio containing a broad mix of assets. Now, thanks to ETFs, someone with a few thousand euros can enjoy the sort of average returns and low risk that previously required millions to produce.

How do you pick an ETF? There are ETFs for large companies, small companies, real investment trusts, international stocks, bonds, even gold. Pick an asset class that is publicly available and you'll find that it is represented by an ETF, or that it will be soon. All the major stock markets have ETFs based on them, for instance.

To learn more about ETFs in general visit Yahoo Finance's ETF Zone (finance.yahoo.com/etf). To learn about Ireland's first ETF, the ISEQ 20 ETF, launched by NCB and managed by Peter Duff, visit its web site (www3.ncbdirect.com). Otherwise you could talk to your stockbroker, your financial adviser or—of course—please do get in touch with me.

Remember, you should always take professional advice before making any financial decision.

(First published 18 March 2007)

46 | FIND IT AND FLIP IT
OFF-PLAN BUYING

You may have heard stories of the fantastic gains to be made buying off-plan. All you have to do is put down a small deposit on a yet-to-be-built property, and then 'flip it'—flipping being the process of selling it on before you have to complete. For instance, you might reserve a €50,000 apartment in a new development in Romania (where property is increasing in value by 25% a year) without ever visiting the site, and before the foundations have even been poured, for as little €2,000. Then, before the apartment is released, you might sell it to someone who lacked the same foresight as yourself for, say, €70,000. The result? An €18,000 capital gain for negligible outlay and negligible risk.

If you think this sounds too good to be true, you would be absolutely right. Unfortunately, unscrupulous and unregulated property promoters make wild and exaggerated claims about buying off-plan, which often result in investors losing tens of thousands of euros. Not that it isn't possible to build a lucrative property empire with the help of some well-chosen off-plan purchases. It is—and it needn't require much capital either—as I will explain in a moment. However, to succeed you need to follow a number of golden rules.

The first step to off-plan profits is to understand the opportunity. For a developer the time between starting a project and completing the final sale can be years. During this period they have to fund the entire cost of building and marketing, and they also face the risk that factors beyond their control (problems with the contractor, falling property prices, rising interest rates, a natural disaster and so forth) will affect their eventual profit. Therefore, with a view to 'locking in' buyers—and as an aid to cash flow— they will sell off some or all of the properties well before they are finished. In order to reward purchasers for committing themselves at this early stage the developer may offer various incentives, usually in the form of a discount on the completion price.

However, in developments that are almost guaranteed to sell out and where prices will almost definitely rise quickly, there may be no incentive other than the certainty of knowing that you will be able to buy your chosen property at the agreed price. Of course, no developer expects you to pay the full price of your property until it is finished. Instead they will ask you to pay a reservation fee (usually no more than a couple of thousand euros, and often less) and, on the exchange of contracts, a deposit. This deposit will be as much as the developer can get away with. The better the development the higher the sum, but a range of 10% to 30% is normal. There are likely to be other costs too, such as survey and legal fees.

So, when you buy off-plan you are, in effect, gaining three money-making advantages. Firstly, you should be achieving a saving on the eventual price. This saving may be worth as little as 5%, but on, say, a €300,000 property that's still €15,000. Secondly, you only have to find a fraction of the eventual price until such time as you complete the purchase. This allows you to gear your investment. Thirdly, you have however long it takes until the property is ready to decide whether to flip it, rent it out or occupy it yourself.

It is the ease with which you can buy off-plan that catches many investors. What they don't realise is that

- you shouldn't exchange on a property unless you have the funds (in other words a mortgage or other finance) to complete; if you don't you could find yourself paying expensive penalties
- you should never assume that you will be able to resell the property before completion
- if you are planning to rent out the property you need to satisfy yourself that the yield will be sufficiently high to cover your mortgage repayments or that you have enough other income to meet any shortfall
- the reservation fee is only the beginning of your expenses. You need to have sufficient cash to cover all the other costs.

It must also be remembered that much can go wrong. The developer may go bankrupt; the development may not meet the intended standards; some unconnected event, such as a stock market crash, may affect demand. There is much you can do, however, to protect yourself against all these eventualities. What's more, when you get it right the rewards are substantial.

If you read my column regularly you may remember, for instance, that a few months ago I spoke in glowing terms of an off-plan opportunity in Granada, Spain. Well, I have come across another excellent Spanish development by the same developers at Jerez de la Frontera, were the sherry comes from. What a beautiful place! You have everything here: the historic city less than five minutes away, a growing airport, golf (eighteen-hole championship course designed by Jack Nicklaus, where negotiations are under way to bring back the Volvo Masters in 2011), great beaches, amazing horse shows from the royal equestrian school (for instance, the dressage Olympic gold medal winner, both horse and rider, came from Jerez). Seville and its airport are a mere forty minutes away.

The development, Altos de Montecastillo, is within the Montecastillo golf resort, the same resort where there are also forty exclusive villas right on the course. These villas are priced at €594,000 upwards. Right above the five-star hotel and club-house are a number of small apartment blocks with stunning views. One-bedroom apartments start at €218,000, two-bedroom apartments at €230,000, with a 15% deposit required initially, followed by a further 5% twelve months later. You pay the balance on completion. In my view, it's well worth a visit to see what all the fuss is about. E-mail me for details.

Which leads me on to the Money Doctor's Golden Off-Plan Profit Rules. These are:

1. Adopt an attitude of healthy scepticism.
2. Get your finance lined up before you start.
3. It is as much about 'location, location, location' as any other property purchase. Only invest in developments that are in prime locations. Never buy 'off plan' unless you—or someone you trust—have inspected the site in person.
4. Check and double-check the credentials of everyone involved: the property investment company (if you are using one), developer, builder and management company. Note that in many countries it is possible to get a completion guarantee underwritten by an insurance company or bank.
5. Research the local market. What are similar properties

selling for? What would a similar property rent for? Don't rely on the developer for this information. Remember too that many developers guarantee the rental income for a couple of years and write it off as a marketing cost.

6. Check that the area has appropriate amenities. In a tourist spot this might mean such things as beaches and restaurants, elsewhere it might mean such things as public transport and schools.

7. Use experienced professionals to advise you.

8. Study the contract closely. If you plan to try to flip the property, watch for restrictions on marketing and advertising that the developer may impose. Investigate the dispute process. Insist that the developer advise you of any changes to the plan. Ascertain what the service charges are likely to be. Make sure you like the way the property is going to be managed.

9. If the developer has started work, ask for an on-site inspection. Otherwise visit one or more of their other developments. Try to obtain referrals from previous purchasers.

Remember, you should always take professional advice before making any financial decision.

(First published 6 May 2007)

47 | SHARE THE WEALTH
HISTORIC SHARE CERTIFICATES

Scripophily, which, as everyone knows, is the collection of old bonds and share certificates, offers investors two distinct profit opportunities. The first and more exciting (albeit improbable) possibility is buying certificates that—despite all appearances to the contrary—are still valid. There was a report in the *Financial Times* last year, for instance, about a collector who spent a few hundred pounds on some share certificates dated 1890 for an English textile company. After doing a little research he found that the company was still trading and that his shares were actually worth £80,000. The second and more certain way of making money is to become a collector.

The size of gains being made by scripophiliacs may surprise you. It is a young market—it is has really only been in existence for thirty years or so—which means that it is still possible to make new discoveries. Unlike, say, philately or numismatics, where it is extremely rare for something 'unknown' to surface, scripophily offers collectors a chance to regularly make important finds. Also, because the number of scripophiliacs is growing dramatically, the market as a whole is moving steadily upwards. Dealers I spoke to were unwilling to be drawn on how fast, but it was generally felt that investors could comfortably achieve 10% a year returns and more, provided they bought well.

The financial aspects aside, it is easy to understand why collectors get bitten by the scripophily bug. To start with, older shares have often been signed in person by well-known figures—everyone from Éamon de Valera to John DeLorean and from King Charles I of England to Walt Disney. Apparently both Truman Capote and Goethe signed share certificates in their day. Then there is the fact that many examples are works of art in their own right, especially those produced between the 1890s and the 1930s. Scripophily is also an excuse to do historical research in a particular era or subject. Finally, there are so many different angles that it isn't difficult to bring together a unique and valuable collection for relatively little money. Remember, until a few years ago old share certificates and bonds were considered curios of little financial worth.

Although the history of shares can be traced back four thousand years, the glory days, so far as scripophiliacs are concerned, began in the late seventeenth century and ended in about 1940. To be collectable, shares and bonds should generally be defunct. This could be for a variety of reasons: governments may have reneged on their bond obligations, companies may have gone into liquidation, or an acquisition or merger may have made the certificates redundant. Some, of course, were printed but never sold; others may have been in safe storage and have only just come to light.

Prices are influenced by a variety of factors, including:

(1) **condition.** Grading is not as strict as it is for stamps or coins. Nevertheless, you should aim to buy only uncirculated (looks like new), extremely fine (slight

traces of wear) or very fine (minor traces of wear) examples.

(2) **rarity.** Generally speaking, the fewer issued the fewer to have survived, or the older the certificate the more valuable it will be.

(3) **historical importance.** Whether issued by companies, political parties or governments, shares and bonds often mark events or movements of significance. The Wright Brothers, for instance, sold shares to fund their experiments with aeroplane manufacture, and Fenian bonds were sold to fund the Irish republican movement.

(4) **age.** Older certificates are usually worth more than later certificates of the same sort. For instance, an early railway share from the 1840s would be worth more than one from the 1850s.

(5) **artistry.** Some collectors are more interested in the decoration and illustration than anything else.

(6) **autograph.** A certificate bearing a famous autograph is always worth more. One of the most expensive share certificates ever sold is for Standard Oil from 1873. Not only was it one of the first oil companies ever floated but the certificates are all signed by John D. Rockefeller. Examples have made $130,000 and more.

What should you collect? As far as I can make out, very few people are investing in Irish share certificates and bonds. Indeed, when I searched the internet the best I could come up with was a single certificate for something called the Connemara Mining Company of Ireland dated 1852, another for Northern Bank from 1929, and the articles of incorporation of the DeLorean Motor Company from 1981 and signed by the man himself. You might also look at some more recent issues—Pixar Animation Studios, peppered with an array of characters from its films, for instance—or maybe some of the iconic brands, such as Harley-Davidson and Coca-Cola. Other possible areas might be companies that went spectacularly bankrupt (Enron shares are now changing hands at $125 each, despite being worthless), frauds, famous transport (such as the White Star Line, which owned the *Titanic*), or shares in high denominations. The latter would mean that, on paper at least, you could become an instant millionaire.

Resources. If you have some old share certificates or bonds and you want to find out if the company is still trading (possibly under a different name) you should ask your stockbroker or try the Companies Registration Office (www.cro.ie or 1890 220226); for Britain, Companies House (www.companies-house.gov.uk); or for the United States, Old Company Research (www.oldcompanyresearch.com).

Become a member of the International Bond and Share Society, which produces directories, newsletters and other useful information. It can also put you in touch with other collectors interested in the same area as yourself (www.scripophily.org).

Search on line for dealers. One of the largest in the world is www.scripophily.com, founded by an American accountant called Bob Kerstein.

Condition is vital to the value of a certificate. Buy items in the best condition you can afford.

Invest in special albums for storing your collection. The wrong plastic or paper can, over time, cause damage.

Certificates will fade if exposed to light, especially sunlight. If you want to decorate your office with certificates, ask the framer to use special glass or acrylic to reduce the effects of sunlight. Bear in mind that if you display a share certificate you may see its value slowly fade in front of your eyes.

Remember, you should always take professional advice before making any financial decision.

(First published 24 June 2007)

48 | WELL ENDOWED
TRADED ENDOWMENT POLICIES

I am about to reveal an investment secret that canny insiders have been using to their financial advantage for years—a secret that could lead you to well-above-average returns with little or no risk.

Only about one out of three endowment policies ever reach maturity. I know, it sounds more like a statistic than a money-making secret, but believe you me it is a piece of information on which fortunes have been founded.

Let me explain. Two out of three people who start long-term savings plans with insurance companies stop them or cash them in well before the agreed term. As a result they miss out on the best bit, because these types of plan are designed with one purpose in mind: to provide the highest possible return on maturity. How is it possible to profit from this fact? By buying up unwanted endowment insurance policies—in other words, taking over a policy that someone else started a few years ago but no longer requires, paying the monthly premiums for the rest of the term, and then scooping the lump sum that is due on maturity.

Second-hand endowments, known in the trade as traded

endowment policies (TEPS), offer you a number of benefits:

- They are an ideal way to build capital for future needs.
- If you know you are going to require money at a specific date—say, to fund third-level education or nursing-home fees—they offer an excellent way to do so.
- Many TEPS were originally taken out to pay off mortgages, and if you have any interest-only loans they are perfect for this purpose.
- It is a good way to expose yourself to the stock market without having to make a direct investment. Some investors use them to achieve portfolio diversity.

With regard to the last point, it is worth noting that when you invest in equity-linked vehicles, such as managed funds or unit trusts, your capital is at risk. If you buy a TEP this is not usually the case, provided you continue to pay the premiums and keep the policy in force until the stated maturity date. Why? Because the basic 'sum assured' and 'annual bonuses' will be 'locked in' (or guaranteed) when you buy your TEP and should be worth more than the purchase price. This risk-free aspect is obviously highly attractive.

You may be wondering at this point why, if endowment policies are such a good investment, the original owners are willing to sell them. There are a variety of reasons why such policies may no longer be relevant to the seller's needs. Maybe it was taken out to back a mortgage; maybe the premiums are more than the policyholder can afford; maybe the policyholder has other, more suitable investment options. Whatever the reason, when you have an unwanted endowment policy you have a number of choices:

- Make the policy 'paid up'. This means that you stop

paying the premiums and simply wait until the maturity date and take your chances on what the return will be.
- Borrow against the policy.
- Surrender the policy to the life assurance company you bought it from.

It usually takes between five and seven years for the surrender value on a policy to be worth the amount of money invested. This is because of the charges, fund management costs and so forth attached to these types of product and because, of course, they are usually designed to run for between twenty and thirty years. Indeed, much of the value of a policy will be in something called the 'terminal bonus'. This is paid on maturity, and although it isn't guaranteed it is likely to represent a large percentage of the policy's return. Terminal bonuses are yet another reason why TEPs make such good investment vehicles. Anyway, from the seller's viewpoint there is no point in accepting a low surrender value when another investor will pay you more to take the policy over.

Obviously, not all TEPs are worth buying, and one option is to ask your independent financial adviser to help you out. In general, you should expect to pay about 10 to 15% over the surrender value offered by the company that issued the policy. For a TEP to be worth investing in, by the way, it should be at least five years old and should have a surrender value of at least €2,500. You will want to know
- the name of the life company and the policy number
- the name and other details of the life assured (the person who owns the policy now)
- the surrender value at a recent date
- what locked-in bonuses there are
- when the policy was started and when it matures

- the basic 'sum assured'
- the gross monthly premiums.

When you buy the policy you will, incidentally, be buying all the benefits, including the life cover. If the original policyholder should die, the money you receive will be the basic sum assured.

The tax position with TEPS will depend on the type of policy and whether you buy here in Ireland or overseas (see below), and you should take specialist advice in this regard. In some circumstances, however, it is possible that your investment may be tax-free or taxed as a capital gain.

How do you set about finding TEPS to purchase? The Irish market is relatively undeveloped, although it is worth searching the internet to see what is available. You may, therefore, be better off looking overseas. If you would prefer to stick to euros then you could try the European Policy Exchange (www.epex-group.com), which specialises in German TEPS. If you would like to buy in US dollars (which certainly represent value for money at the moment) then you will be interested in something called the 'secondary life insurance market'. One of the longest-established players is Life Partners Inc. (www.lifepartners inc.com). The British market is highly developed, and the Association of Policy Market Makers (www.apmm.co.uk) lists six different specialist brokers on its web site. In Ireland the leader in this market is www.ifggroup.com. For further details, e-mail me directly.

Remember, you should always take professional advice before making any financial decision.

(First published 3 June 2007)

49 | **MERCURY RISING**
ALCHEMY—BASE METALS TO GOLD

If you had bought €10,000 worth of the metal molybdenum—it gets added to steel during the smelting process—in 2003, your little cache would have been worth a cool €1,000,000 by 2005. For anyone interested in high-risk, high-return investments, metals—and in particular minor metals—offer jaw-dropping returns. A 1,000% gain is exceptional but not untypical of the sort of super-profits that can be made in this sector.

Before I tantalise you with other mouth-watering examples (even boring old copper turned €1,000 into €1,480 in sixty days earlier this year), let me stress that you shouldn't even think of investing in metals unless you have already built up a diversified portfolio of more traditional assets. If you have bought property, sorted out a decent pension and otherwise been sensible with your cash, then—and only then—should you consider putting a modest amount of money—money you can afford to lose—into something metallic.

There are three influences on metal prices: supply, demand and speculation. This is best explained with a case history. Over the last five years nickel prices have risen by roughly 600%. Why? Nickel is used in stainless steel, for which demand has been steadily increasing, especially in China, where production grew by 68% in 2006. This has resulted in stockpiles being depleted—by 90% in the last year alone, to near fifteen-year lows and less than one day of global consumption. Manufacturers, nervous that they will have to pay even more for supplies in the future, have been buying, pushing the price up. Speculators, smelling an opportunity for gain, have been following suit.

What has been happening to nickel has also been happening to other, less well-known metals. Alex Heath, who heads the base metals trading team at RBC Capital, was recently quoted by Bloomberg as saying: 'It's no surprise that minor metals are rising in this fashion because they are in genuine shortage and buyers want to know whether they will be able to source material.' When a metal becomes scarce, mining companies begin to consider whether it is worth extracting more from existing mines or exploring for new sources. Obviously they don't want to gear up production, which may take years and is costly, only to find that there is an over-supply. Equally, they don't want to miss out on a profit opportunity. Trying to gauge what will happen to supplies is a major factor when weighing up the relative prospects of different metals.

So what should you invest in, and when? One of the attractive aspects of the minor metals—by which I mean metals that aren't traded on the major exchanges—is that private and even professional investors largely ignore them. This means that with careful research it is possible to spot opportunities that the market as a whole may miss—opportunities such as

beryllium—which is used to make speciality alloys for electronics, defence applications and the automotive industry. There are very few active mines in the world and 65% of reserves are found in the United States.

bismuth—a non-toxic lead substitute that can be used as a steel additive. It is a by-product of lead ore, and because lead production levels have been low, supplies have been run down.

chromium—a component of stainless steel and super-alloys. It has benefited from the strength of the global steel market. If the price falls, then higher-cost producers are likely to 'shut their doors,' thus tightening supply.

manganese—another steel additive and another metal that has benefited from the global demand for steel.

selenium—used as an additive in glass, as a dietary supplement and in alloys. It is largely a by-product of zinc and copper mining. As a result of recent increases in copper prices more selenium is coming on stream. Nevertheless, it is to be remembered that between 2003 and 2005 the metal enjoyed an 800% increase, and some investors will undoubtedly buy again if the price falls dramatically, in the hope of a repeat performance.

vanadium—used in metallurgical applications. It showed a staggering 1,542% gain between 2002 and 2005, because two of the world's largest producers closed their mines, sparking a severe shortage. As it is often found within uranium deposits, if uranium prices rise, vanadium prices are likely to fall.

There are rhodium and gallium, thorium and osmium, antimony and tungsten—the list of possibilities seems almost endless. A canny investor narrows it down by

- sticking to metals that have a reasonably sized market. If only a few million dollars' worth of a metal gets bought and sold each year, and if there aren't recognised exchanges, it will be hard to trade.
- choosing metals that aren't too dependent on outside

factors. Any metal linked to steel production, for instance, is going to be vulnerable if there's a downturn in the economy. A metal such as antimony or selenium has wider applications.

- thinking mid to long-term. It isn't where prices are today that is important, it is where they are going to be in a few months and a few years.
- picking minor metals that are by-products of larger-market metals, such as copper, and investing in mining companies that produce both. This helps to reduce risk.

There is a range of investment options. The last thing you want is to take physical delivery of any metal, as this would require storage, insurance and transport costs. If you are investing a sizeable sum you could hunt out publicly quoted mining companies that specialise in your chosen metal and buy their shares direct. If you are investing a more modest sum there are various managed funds and even exchange-traded funds (ETFS) on offer. There aren't many legal investment opportunities in the world that can show the sort of gains that minor metals can offer. But if you want to be a successful metal detector, do your homework first.

Remember, you should always take professional advice before making any financial decision.

(First published 10 June 2007)

50 | **PLASTIC FANTASTIC**
PLASTICS

My favourite piece of dialogue from the film classic *The Graduate* (1967) is when Mr McGuire (Walter Brooke) offers Benjamin Braddock (Dustin Hoffman) some career advice.

Mr McGuire: I want to say one word to you. Just one word.

Benjamin: Yes, sir.

Mr McGuire: Are you listening?

Benjamin: Yes, I am.

Mr McGuire: Plastics.

Forty years later, Mr McGuire's advice is looking increasingly topical. Plastic—in its various guises—is the hot new commodity on the block, and anyone interested in an investment that is likely to give the flattest of portfolios a bit of bounce would do well to consider its potential.

What sort of potential? The main chemicals used in plastic manufacture have been rising by between 20% and 70% per annum in recent years. While it would be hard for a private investor to plug in to those sorts of gains without undue risk, it gives you an idea of why plastic is looking especially fantastic right now.

As you may remember from your chemistry class in school, plastics are just one class of man-made polymeric material (naturally occurring examples of polymers include starch and cellulose), and they fall into two basic categories: thermoplastics and thermosets. Thermoplastics soften with the application of heat and can be injected into moulds and then cooled to form shapes. Examples include bottles, bags, drums and pipes. They can be made from a range of materials, including polyethylene, polypropylene, PVC and PET. Thermosets are rather more sophisticated, as they contain a setting mechanism that allows them to be shaped by hardening using a chemical reaction. Examples include the advanced composite fuselage of high-tech planes and a modern tennis racquet frame. The word 'plastic', by the way, comes from the Greek for 'to form.'

The interesting thing about plastics from an investment viewpoint is that world consumption is now growing faster than for the closest equivalent commodity—metals. World sales of thermoplastics alone are $120 billion a year—more than the total value of all non-precious metal sales.

This isn't hard to understand when you think of all the different sectors that depend on plastics, from transport and packaging to consumer durables and textiles. Building, medical goods and agriculture alone account for tens of billions of euros in sales a year. As demand soars, so does the need for the various chemicals—such as ethylene, polyethylene and chlorine—used in producing plastic.

Take ethylene. Since 2003 demand has grown by 5% a year, but, because of world shortages, prices have grown by 20% a year. Polyethylene resin, incidentally, showed 30% a year price gains over the same period. Little wonder that in 2005 the London Metals Exchange launched two special plastics futures contracts. Such contracts allow manufacturers to protect themselves from price increases.

What about the potential risks? First of all, a large percentage of polyethylene is used in house building and car manufacturing, meaning that any downturn in the global economy will hit demand. Secondly, a seventh of the world's plastic output is being consumed by China. So, any change in the Chinese economy could have a disproportionate effect on prices. Thirdly, because crude oil and natural gas are the main ingredients in plastics, higher fuel prices mean higher plastic prices. This is not, as one might expect, automatically good news for chemical and plastics companies, as the final users are not always willing to absorb these additional costs. Finally, although it is a long way off, there is a move away from traditional plastics to more environmentally responsible materials. I've written in the past about the development of natural plastics, using such materials as corn syrup, and in time such products are likely to have an effect on the market.

Nevertheless, despite all the potential risks there is no getting around the fact that vast quantities of plastics are going to be consumed for the foreseeable future, making it as sensible, if not more sensible, an investment than many of the obvious options—especially as, with a bit of cunning, it should be possible to insulate oneself from the worst hazards.

Here are some different ideas:

- Consider buying directly into companies producing the raw materials that are used in plastic. You might look at such firms as Dow Chemicals, Innovene Europe and Reliance Industries of India. In the United States you might put your money into more specialist companies, such as Lyondell Chemical (ethylene), Nova Chemicals (ethylene), Olin Corporation (chlor-alkalis) or PPG Industries (chlor-alkalis). The Middle East is in the process of developing a number of new chemical plants that use natural gas to produce ethylene and other plastic ingredients. Thanks to lower labour costs, the companies behind these plants are likely to enter the market with a price advantage. A good group to look at there might be Sabic.

- Pick one of the many managed funds and ETFs that specialise in petrochemical businesses.
- Make a more creative investment. For example, invest in the shares of a firm called Plastic Logic, a company that hopes to replace conventional silicone semiconductors with a plastic alternative. They've already developed an infinitely cheaper microchip and are now building a factory in Germany that should go into production in 2008.
- For a greener investment option, several of the chemical companies and agricultural processors have started to use corn, vegetable oil and other raw materials to create bio-based chemicals and plastics. Biotech firms such as Biofine, Carghill, Codexis, Diversa, Dyadic International and Genencor use genetic engineering to produce superenzymes and bacteria that, in turn, can turn corn into plastics.

Making money is about looking into the future, anticipating trends before they happen. If you want to invest in an area that is likely to show long-term growth, then Mr McGuire was undoubtedly right. In a word: plastics.

Remember, you should always take professional advice before making any financial decision.

(First published 8 July 2007)

INDEX